SCHADENFREUDE

SCHADENFREUDE

The Joy of Another's Misfortune

Tiffany Watt Smith

Little, Brown Spark
New York Boston London

Little, Brown Spark
Hachette Book Group
1290 Avenue of the Americas, New York, NY 10104
littlebrownspark.com

First North American Edition: November 2018
Originally published in Great Britain by Profile Books in partnership with Wellcome Collection, October 2018

Little, Brown Spark is an imprint of Little, Brown and Company, a division of Hachette Book Group, Inc. The Little, Brown Spark name and logo are trademarks of Hachette Book Group, Inc.

The Hachette Speakers Bureau provides a wide range of authors for speaking events. To find out more, go to hachettespeakersbureau.com or call (866) 376-6591.

10 9 8 7 6 5 4 3 2 1

ISBN 978-0-316-47030-8
LCCN 2018939521

LSC-C

Printed in the United States of America

To my brother, Tom

"The blessed in the kingdom of heaven will see the punishments of the damned, so that their bliss will be that much greater."

—St. Thomas Aquinas, *Summa Theologiae*, written 1265–1274

Contents

Prologue A Community of the Failed   1

1: Accidents   19
2: Glory   33
3: Justice   45
4: The Smug   59
5: Love   75
6: Envy   93
7: Mutiny   107
8: Power   121

Afterword Schadenfreude:
The Rules of Engagement   137

Acknowledgments   145
Referenced Works   147

An Index of Schadenfreude: A select catalog
of its variations, causes and consequences   155

Times I feel pleased at things going wrong for other people:

When a news correspondent gets tangled up in her scarf in strong winds on live TV.

Seeing an urban unicyclist almost collide with a parked car.

At the shops, when the person in front of me is rude to the cashier and then their card is declined.

When I hear about satnavs sending lorries down narrow country lanes where they get stuck.

When my coworker was training for a marathon, boring us all with his training plans and special diet, ostentatiously checking his Fitbit and tweeting his stats, wearing his tiny, shiny red running shorts into work, festooning said shorts over his desk chair to dry, stretching by the photocopier, talking about his groin injury, always smelling of sweat and then not completing his marathon.

Tattoo fails (no regerts!).

And once, in my twenties, when my effortlessly attractive friend got dumped.

A Community of the Failed

Last Tuesday, I went to the corner shop to buy milk, and found myself pausing by the celebrity gossip magazines. And my first instinct, just in case someone was listening in on my thoughts, was to think: *ugh, who buys those terrible magazines*. But then I picked one up, *just out of curiosity*. There was the cellulite, the weight gain and loss, the bikinis riding up between the bum cheeks and bingo wings circled in red. My favorite story was an interview with a pop star, or perhaps she was a model, who lived in a giant luxury mansion. Now I'm the sort of person who usually curdles with envy on hearing about someone else's luxury mansion. But this was different. The story was about how she was lonely. Tragically lonely following a tragic breakup.

I looked about, took the magazine to the till and counted out my change. There was a warm sensation working its way across my chest. I felt lucky. No, that's not it. I felt smug.

This is a confession. I love daytime TV. I smoke, even though I officially gave up years ago. I'm often late, and usually lie about why. And sometimes I feel good when others feel bad.

WHAT IS SCHADENFREUDE?

The boss calling himself "Head of Pubic Services" on an important letter.

Celebrity Vegan Caught in Cheese Aisle.

When synchronized swimmers get confused, swivel the wrong way, and then have *to swivel back really quickly and hope no one notices.*

The Japanese have a saying: "The misfortunes of others taste like honey." The French speak of *joie maligne*, a diabolical delight in other people's suffering. The Danish talk of *skadefryd*, and the Dutch of *leedvermaak*. In Hebrew enjoying other people's catastrophes is *simcha la-ed*, in Mandarin *xìng-zāi-lè-huò*, in Serbo-Croat it is *zlùradòst* and in Russian *zloradstvo*. More than two thousand years ago, Romans spoke of *malevolentia*. Earlier still, the Greeks described *epichairekakia* (literally *epi*, over, *chairo*, rejoice, *kakia*, disgrace). "To see others suffer does one good," wrote the philosopher Friedrich Nietzsche. "To make others suffer even more so. This is a hard saying, but a mighty, human, all-too-human principle."

For the Melanesians who live on the remote Nissan Atoll in Papua New Guinea, laughing at other people's pain is known as "Banbanam." At its most extreme, it involves taunting a dead rival by exhuming their corpse and scattering the remains around the village. More of an everyday sort of Banbanam is gloating at someone's humiliating failure behind their back—as when the rival villagers' feast day is rained on because their Weather Magician's spells fail, or a wife grabs her cheating husband by the testicles and ignores his pleas for mercy. Banbanam is a kind of resistance too. Melanesians still enjoy telling the story of how an Australian government minister visited the village, got annoyed because the villagers wouldn't do what he wanted, drove away in a huff and crashed into a tree.

In historical portraits, people beaming with joy look very different to those slyly gloating over another's bad luck. However, in a laboratory in Würzburg in Germany in 2015, thirty-two football fans agreed to have electromyography pads attached to their faces, which would measure their smiles and frowns while watching TV clips of successful and unsuccessful football penalties by the German team, and by their archrivals, the Dutch. The psychologists found that when the Dutch missed a goal, the German fans' smiles appeared more quickly and were broader than when the German team scored a goal themselves. The smiles of Schadenfreude and joy are indistinguishable except in one crucial respect: we smile more with the failures of our enemies than at our own success.

Make no mistake. Over time, and in many different places, when it comes to making ourselves happy, we humans have long relied on the humiliations and failures of other people.

There has never really been a word for these grubby delights in English. In the 1500s, someone attempted to introduce "epicaricacy" from the ancient Greek, but it didn't catch on. In 1640, the philosopher Thomas Hobbes wrote a list of human passions, and concluded it with a handful of obscure feelings which "want names." "From what passion proceedeth it," he asked, "that men take pleasure to behold from the shore the danger of them that are at sea in a tempest?" What strange combination of joy and pity, he wrote, makes people "content to be spectators of the misery of their friends"? Hobbes's mysterious and terrible passion remained without a name, in the English language at least. In 1926, a journalist in *The Spectator* asserted that "there is no English word for Schadenfreude because there is no such feeling here." He was wrong, of course.

I'm British, and enjoying other people's mishaps and misery feels as much part of my culture as teabags and talking about the weather. "For what do we live but to make sport for our neighbors, and laugh at them in our turn," proclaims Mr. Bennet in that most beloved, apparently quintessentially English of novels, *Pride and Prejudice*. Nothing unites us more strongly in self-righteous joy than an MP caught cooking the books. We're even not averse to a little Schadenfreude at our own expense: as George Orwell once remarked, the English are unique for celebrating not military triumphs, but disasters ("Into the valley of death...").

We know how to enjoy failures. But ask us to name this enjoyment, and our language falls into a hypocritical silence. It averts its gaze and squirms a little.

And so we adopted the German word *Schadenfreude*. From *Schaden,* meaning damage or harm, and *freude*, meaning joy or pleasure: damage-joy.

No one likes to think about their flaws, but in them so much of what makes us human is revealed. Enjoying other people's misfortunes might sound simple—a mere glint of malice, a flick of spite. But look closer, and you'll glimpse some of the most hidden yet important parts of our lives.

When I pay attention to the pleasures I might feel in other people's disasters, I am struck by the variety of tastes and textures involved. There is the glee felt at incompetence—not just of skiers face-planting in the snow, but at screwups of implausible magnitude:

> *When NASA lost a $125 million Mars orbiter*
> *because half the team were using imperial*
> *measurements, and the other, metric.*

And then there is the self-righteous satisfaction I get when hypocrites are exposed:

> *Politician accidentally tweets picture of his erection*
> *(he meant to send it directly to his intern).*

And of course, there is the inner triumph of seeing a rival falter. The other day, in the campus coffee shop, a colleague asked if I'd got the promotion I'd gone for. *No*, I said. And I noticed, at the corner of his mouth, the barely perceptible twitch of a grin before the tumble of commiserations. *Oh bad luck. Ah, their loss, the idiots.* And I was tempted to ask: *Did you just smile?* But I didn't. Because when he loses out—as he sometimes does—I know I experience a happy twinge too.

Sometimes it is easy to share our delight, scoffing at the humiliation of the TV talent show contestant, reposting memes of a disgraced politician's resignation speech, or sharing barely·suppressed glee with our fellow classmates when the teacher farts.

Far harder to acknowledge, even to ourselves, are those spasms of relief which accompany the bad news of our annoyingly successful friends and relatives. They come involuntarily, these confusing bursts of pleasure, swirled through with shame. And they worry us—not just because we may fear that our lack of compassion says something terrible about us, but because they point so clearly to our envy and inferiority, and the way that we eagerly clutch at the disappointments of others in order to feel better about our own:

> *When my brother took his kids on a fabulous*
> *summer holiday to America, I felt bad because I*
> *never take my kids anywhere since it's too much*
> *effort and too expensive. And then I saw his*
> *Facebook status: it rained.*

Today, Schadenfreude is all around us. It's there in the way we do politics, how we treat celebrities, in online fail videos. But these heady pleasures are shot through with unease. Moralists have long despised Schadenfreude. The philosopher Arthur Schopenhauer called it "an infallible sign of a thoroughly bad heart and profound moral worthlessness," the very worst trait in human nature. (He also said that anyone caught enjoying the suffering of others should be shunned from human society. Which made me sweat a bit.)

I have come to believe that Schopenhauer was wrong. We might worry that a taste for other people's misery will corrupt our souls, yet this emotion is far from simply "bad." It touches on things that have mattered most to human societies for millennia: our instincts for fairness and hatred of hypocrisy; our love of seeing our rival suffer in the hope that we might win ourselves; our itch to measure ourselves against others and make sense of our choices when we fall short; how we bond with each other; what makes us laugh.

If we peer more closely at this hidden and much-maligned emotion, liberate ourselves from its shame and secrecy, we will discover a great deal about who we really are.

MALICIOUS DELIGHTS

*When squirrels in my garden forget where
they've buried their nuts.*

*When aggressive van drivers get flashed
by speed cameras.*

*When my three-year-old gloats about how she's got the
last biscuit nah-nah-nah-nah-nah, and is waving it
around, and then our dog snatches it out of her hand.*

When the word *Schadenfreude* first appeared in English writing in 1853, it caused great excitement. This was probably not the intention of R. C. Trench, the Archbishop of Dublin, who mentioned it in his bestselling book on philology, *On the Study of Words*. For Trench, the mere existence of the word *Schadenfreude* was unholy and fearful, a "mournful record of the strange wickednesses which the genius of man, so fertile in evil, has invented."

His fellow Victorians, however, were not so easily put off, and eagerly adopted the word, associating it with a range of pleasures, from hilarity to self-righteous vindication, from triumph to relief. In 1867, Thomas Carlyle, historian and hard-line social commentator, admitted feeling a juicy, if unpatriotic, Schadenfreude ("a secret satisfaction, of the malicious or even of the judiciary kind"), imagining the chaos he hoped would be caused by the passing of the Electoral Reform Act, which gave the vote to some working-class men. In 1881, a chess columnist advised persuading naïve opponents to use a tricky strategy, just to "indulge in what the Germans call 'Schadenfreude'" when they invariably floundered. In the 1890s, animal-rights campaigner Frances Power Cobbe wrote a whole manifesto entitled "Schadenfreude," identifying the emotion with the bloodlust of boys torturing stray cats for fun. And, like us, Victorians were fond of seeing superior people get their comeuppance. The physician Sir William Gull was a pioneer of the healthy living movement in Victorian England, a "water drinker" and a vegetarian (almost). He went about giving self-righteous talks about how his lifestyle would protect him from diseases. So when in 1887 it emerged that he had become seriously ill... Well, reported the *Sheffield and Rotherham Independent* gleefully, there was "a certain amount of what the Germans call Schadenfreude" among advocates of "fuller diet and freer living."

Today we still associate many different pleasures with this

word, unclear perhaps exactly what it means in the original, or where its perimeters lie. But looking at how the word has been used in English, it is possible to identify five repeated themes.

The first is that Schadenfreude is usually thought an opportunistic pleasure, a spectator sport, felt when we stumble across another's misfortune *which we have not caused ourselves*. The Hollywood villain gloating when Bond is caught by his dastardly plot is not experiencing Schadenfreude, but sadistic pleasure. By contrast, the sidekick who sniggers as a Hollywood villain is accidentally foiled by his *own* dastardly plot when he trips and presses the self-destruct button *is* enjoying Schadenfreude.

The second is that Schadenfreude is usually thought of as a furtive emotion, and no wonder. Outbursts of merriment at another's catastrophes are generally a sign of great villainy. Shylock can barely contain himself on learning that his rival Antonio has lost a cargo ship at sea: "I thank God, I thank God. Is't true, is't true?"; "good news, good news!" We might be worried not just about looking malicious, but that our Schadenfreude exposes our other flaws too—our pettiness, our envy, our feelings of inadequacy.

However, the third feature of Schadenfreude is that we often feel entitled to it when the other person's suffering can be construed as a comeuppance—a deserved punishment for being smug or hypocritical, or breaking the law. While it is unlikely that we'd enjoy our moral superiority to their face, gloating is generally permissible at a safe distance. In 2015, U.S. pastor Tony Perkins said that floods were sent by God to punish abortion and gay marriage. And then his own house flooded and he had to escape *in a canoe*. Even the ever-impartial BBC relished this story, posting aerial pictures of the flooded house next to his controversial "God is trying to send us a message" interview.

Fourth, we tend to see Schadenfreude as a form of respite—the failures of others appease our own envy and inadequacy, and give us a much-needed glimpse of superiority. It says as much about our own vulnerabilities as our attitudes to the behavior of others. And just as satire is only funny when it punches up, we are most comfortable sniggering at the failures of those more wealthy, attractive and talented than us. As the philosopher Friedrich Nietzsche, one of the great theorists of this emotion, argued, Schadenfreude is "the revenge of the impotent."

Fifth and finally, Schadenfreude is usually thought of as glee at minor discomforts and gaffes rather than at dire tragedies and deaths (and we usually only think high-order villains are capable of applauding someone's death). But this rule isn't hard and fast, and context matters. We are willing to see celebrities, or people from the remote past, endure horrors that would dismay us if they were happening now or to our friends. All emotions are what psychologists call "cognitive"—in other words, not simply reflex reactions to external triggers, but complex processes requiring us to appraise and judge our relationship with the world around us and tailor our responses accordingly.

Sometimes we judge wrongly, and our Schadenfreude leaves us feeling morally awkward. There is an episode of *The Simpsons* in which Homer's infuriatingly perfect neighbor Ned Flanders opens a shop, The Leftorium. Given the chance to imagine three wishes, Homer fantasizes that Ned's business collapses. First, he sees the shop empty of customers, then Flanders turning out his pockets, then Flanders begging the bailiffs. It is only when Homer imagines Flanders's grave, Flanders's children weeping beside it, that he stops himself. "Too far," he says, and quickly rewinds to the image of the bankrupt shop.

These questions about how and why we enjoy the pain of others — and what is acceptable and what is "too far" — have featured in some of the greatest works of philosophy and literature for over two thousand years. But arguably the urgency to understand Schadenfreude has never been so great as today.

AN AGE OF SCHADENFREUDE

Leotard-wearing contestants in a Japanese game show attempt to scale an inflatable water slide, and keep falling down on top of each other.

Millionaire media star and lifestyle guru jailed for insider trading.

"You won't believe what these child celebrities look like now! (Number 2 will shock you!)."

In December 2008, a reader of the *New York Times* lamented that we are living in a "Golden Age of Schadenfreude." Similar phrases appeared on blogs and in op-eds, crossing continents. "We are living in an Age of Schadenfreude," proclaimed a comment writer in *The Guardian*, a "Spitegeist." Were they right?

They blamed the online babble and our hunger for celebrity meltdowns, and flickering sidebars of shame. They pointed to the malicious behavior of trolls, to the stampedes of public shaming and moral indignation online. They looked at all that showing off on Instagram and said we were succumbing to envy so deep that our only respite was to see people failing bigger and better. More recently, our appetite for Schadenfreude has been held accountable for political shocks on both sides of the Atlantic, driving the consumption of "fake news," and feeding the algorithms which offer up ever more bizarre and titillating transgressions: "Clintons in threesome with their illegal maid!" Could our delight in other people's humiliations be not just a private moral failing, but a public menace?

As a historian of emotions, I have seen this sort of thing before. There were many instances in the past when people declared themselves living through a period dominated by some emotion or another: eighteenth-century writers spoke of an outpouring of sympathy and kindness in their time; in the 1940s, W. H. Auden described an "Age of Anxiety." Such labels might seem to signal a sudden and bizarre outbreak of contagious feeling, but in practice, they are the focal point around which all kinds of other desires and fears coalesce. For example, during the nineteenth century, there was a great deal of enthusiasm for self-improvement and productivity — and in turn, a sudden unease about their opposite, boredom. Doctors started writing articles about its dangers (which ran from alcoholism to onanism). Politicians jumped on the band-wagon, and started blaming the unemployed and poor for infecting others with idleness. For feminists, boredom was a threat to wealthy women; moralists feared it would turn children to wanton cruelties. As Charles Dickens wryly put it, boredom had become "the chronic malady of our times."

Truthfully, we can't ever know whether we are actually experiencing more Schadenfreude today than ever before. It certainly *seems* more of an obvious feature of our collective lives, since what used to be hidden or else communicated in fleeting sniggers by the water cooler is now preserved forever in "likes" and "shares" in the digital aspic.

But there is certainly the moral frenzy. Remember when Kim Kardashian was robbed in Paris, with millions of dollars of jewelry stolen (including a ridiculous diamond ring she'd been flaunting on Instagram a few days earlier)? When the BBC reported the robbery, they included a tweet by British comedian James Corden urging people to stop joking about it on Twitter. I immediately clicked on the thread (*for research!*). But to me, it looked like the volume of jokes was matched by that of tweets by indignant Twitter users telling off other Twitter users for being mean. We are immensely conflicted about Schadenfreude, unsure what pains we are "allowed" to enjoy, and where our scoffing will cause too much hurt. On the one hand, gossip sites and tabloid rags encourage us to indulge; on the other, we are condemned when we do.

There has also been an explosion of research. Before 2000,

barely any academic articles were published with the word *Schaden-freude* in the title. Now, even the most cursory search throws up hundreds, from neuroscience to philosophy to management studies. They range from experiments on children willing to pay good money to see puppets punished, to studies of how PR firms manipulate Schadenfreude when a rival's product fails. Many of the insights gleaned from these studies are discussed in this book. But their timing and volume is just as revealing, evidence that this emotion has caught our attention today with an intensity it never had before.

What is driving all this interest in Schadenfreude? No doubt, it is partly motivated by our attempts to understand life in the online world, where sniggering at other people, once often socially inappropriate, now comes with less risk. Just as important, in my view, is our growing commitment to empathy. The capacity to attune ourselves to other people's suffering is highly prized today — and rightly so. Putting ourselves in another's shoes impacts on our ability to lead others, to parent, to be a decent partner and friend. Yet the more important empathy becomes, the more obnoxious Schadenfreude seems.

It is not just Victorian moralists who recoil from Schadenfreude. Twenty-first-century humanists who regard empathy as a "natural" response under threat in a frenetic, atomistic modern world find it awkward too. Schadenfreude has variously been called the "absence of empathy," the "opposite of empathy" and "empathy's shadow," casting the two as fundamentally incompatible. The psychologist Simon Baron-Cohen has pointed out that psychopaths are not only detached from other people's suffering but might even enjoy it: "The Germans have a word for this," writes Baron-Cohen, "*Schadenfreude*." With all this swirling around, it's little wonder that even when Schadenfreude feels right, it also feels very wrong indeed.

But of course, laughing at Wile E. Coyote flattened by an Acme anvil or feeling a sudden dart of pleasure that your sister's new perm (*that she'd been going on about for weeks*) did not go exactly to plan does not make you a monster. Few of us enjoy other people's pain for its own sake, but more often because we have judged it deserved or useful in some way, evidence not strictly of malice but of our desire to preserve a moral balance. Of course, Schadenfreude has its benefits: a quick win which alleviates inferiority or envy; a way of bonding over the failure of a boss or smug senior colleague.

And above all, Schadenfreude is a testament to our capacity for emotional flexibility, as opposed to moral rigidity, and our ability to hold apparently contradictory thoughts and feelings in mind simultaneously. Schadenfreude and sympathy are not either/or responses as is sometimes suggested, but can be felt all at once. Dostoyevsky knew this. When, in *Crime and Punishment*, Marmeladov is brought, bloodied and unconscious, into the St. Petersburg tenement where he lives following an accident, all the residents crowd round. They experience, wrote Dostoyevsky, "that strange sense of inner satisfaction that always manifests itself, even among the victim's nearest and dearest, when someone is afflicted by a sudden catastrophe; a sensation that not a single one of us is proof against, however sincere our feelings of pity and sympathy."

We may well be living in an Age of Schadenfreude, and fear

that this emotion is leading us astray. But as with all emotions, condemning it only gets you so far. What we really need is to think afresh about the work this much-maligned emotion does for us, and what it tells us about our relationships with ourselves and each other.

SCHADENFREUDE: A CELEBRATION

When a casino magnate put his elbow through a $48.4 million painting by Picasso (that he was just about to sell).

When you discover your ex's off-again on-again fiancée is marrying somebody else.

Horse yoga (in which people do yoga on top of horses) and when it goes wrong.

In writing this book, I have watched more clips of cats falling off walls than is sensible, and roamed around corners of the Internet that I have no desire to revisit. But I have also read countless articles, spoken to neuroscientists and psychologists, legal scholars and philosophers, discussed sibling rivalry with an agony aunt, envy with my friends and sniggering babies with a psychologist, and have found that Schadenfreude is a much larger part of my life than I had previously been comfortable admitting.

This book explores many interconnected species of Schadenfreude, each with its illicit pleasure to be savored. Each chapter will deal with a different aspect of Schadenfreude, from the giddy excitement of seeing ridiculous accidents to the satisfactions of seeing criminals brought to justice, from the secret relief of seeing a horribly successful friend falter to mass rejoicing when a political enemy implodes. And if by the end of reading all this you feel a little gray around the gills at how much Schadenfreude *you* feel, in the afterword I offer some "Rules of Engagement" for how to deal with your shameful Schadenfreude—and far more importantly, what to do when you catch someone else feeling it at your expense.

This book is motivated not by questions of what we should or shouldn't feel, but by a desire to understand why we experience pleasure at other people's misfortunes at all, and what it feels like when we do.

In writing it, what seemed at first to me to be a minor grace note revealed itself as a major chord in my life. And what seemed peripheral or inconsequential emerged as a truly significant part of the way we relate to one another and ourselves. Schadenfreude may appear antisocial. Yet it is a feature of many of our most cherished communal rituals, from sports to gossip. It may seem misanthropic, yet it is enmeshed in so much of what is distinctly human about how we live: the instinct for justice and fairness; a need for hierarchies and the quest for status within them; the desire to belong to and protect the groups that keep us safe. It may seem superior and demeaning, yet it also speaks of our need to appreciate the absurdity of our attempts to appear in control in a world forever slipping out of our grasp. It might seem isolating and divisive, but it also testifies to our need to not feel alone in our disappointments, but to seek the consolations of being part of a community of the failed.

Schadenfreude, exultant, exquisite and utterly shabby, is a flaw, granted. But it is the flaw we must face up to if we truly want to understand life in the modern world.

Accidents

Falling over, diarrhea and other disasters

Tree surgeon saws through the branch he's sitting on.

Trousers fall down during tea with the vicar.

*Woman sneezes while adding final touches
to house of cards.*

In the weeks after my second child was born, when I was half delirious with sleeplessness and pinned to the sofa by a snoozing baby, a video appeared on my Facebook feed. It was called "Man Jumps into Frozen Pool." It had over four million views. I clicked play.

Imagine the scene: a back garden in Germany, or Lithuania or somewhere. The air is misty. There is a rockery, some fir trees, a short jetty leading to a swimming pool, its water so cold that it seems to have frosted over in patches. A muscly guy in his early twenties wearing a black speedo stands barefoot on a rock, shivering and hugging his chest. He appears to be psyching himself up to jump in. Then he turns to the camera, kneels, gives the rock metal salute (the hand horn: index finger and pinky up, middle fingers down), gives his best gangsta monologue in what appears to be some combination of German and English, and then runs across the jetty and cannonballs into the water. But there isn't any water. It's just thick, hard ice, and he lands smack on his arse and skids across it.

I tried stifling my giggles so I wouldn't wake the baby in my arms. I shook and snorted. I must have appeared like someone having a particularly weird seizure. I was in pain from laughing, but I didn't care. I watched that video again and again. "Man Jumps into Frozen Pool" made me feel euphoric.

It didn't take long for me to start roaming around the Internet for more. I googled "Fail Videos," "Epic Fail Videos," "Best of Epic Fail Videos," "Faceplants," "Bloopers," "Epic Faceplants." The best of these collections would run for ten minutes or so. They would feature keep-fit enthusiasts bouncing right off their trampolines and into the nearest hedge, grooms farting during the vows, glamorous TV presenters tumbling backward over their sofas and security cam footage of people texting who walk head-first into shopping mall fountains and bus shelters. I became au fait with the subcategories: "terrible drivers," "spray tan disasters," "YOU ONLY HAD ONE JOB"…

In these odd early weeks, where nights and days were indistinguishable, these videos were my secret, my salvation.

There is a difference between fail videos and slapstick, don't get me wrong. And there were nights when I turned to the latter, thinking it more highbrow and edifying. I rediscovered my love for the beautiful, solemn Buster Keaton, and sighed with pleasure as he battled cyclones and dodged collapsing buildings, only to be knocked out by a flying cardboard box. I snorted watching Laurel and Hardy spend hours maneuvering a piano up to the top of a staircase, only for it to fall all the way back down again. I put the "Make 'Em Laugh" sequence from *Singin' in the Rain* on repeat, and surrendered to the clockwork perfection of its pratfalls and backflips.

But these were all stunts. No match for the cheap thrill of people really dropping priceless ornaments or being menaced by ostriches or chased by bees. The bloopers kept drawing me back. I craved bigger and better.

Reading the comments, I could see people got very exercised about whether a fail was genuine, their gaze sharpened for clues — a quick glance to the camera, a sense of preparedness. Even the faintest whiff of a setup was met with scorn, not just for the people who made the video in a cynical bid for viral fame and cash, but for those viewers who had been taken in. What excited the fail connoisseurs was not so much that another person had experienced something really painful, but the fact that they were not expecting it. It was the surprise of it. The sense that a person had been undone.

LAUGHTER

Fail videos are the cultural pinnacle of our Age of Schaden-freude. Let's be clear about their popularity. The most-watched TED talks—inspiring talks about education, leadership and cre-ativity, by global leaders and Harvard academics—currently clock around 30 million views. A clip of a dad being kicked in the nuts by his toddler daughter has been watched by over 256 million peo-ple around the world (so far). Perhaps you find this dispiriting.

But these pleasures are not new, or an invention of the Internet. Before fail videos, there was *You've Been Framed* and *America's Funniest Home Videos*. And before home video cameras, there were letters, diaries and pranks. In the third century AD, the emperor Elagabalus liked to sit some of his dinner guests on airbags, which then deflated so they fell under the table. There is an ancient Egyp-tian tomb from the fifteenth century BC that depicts one of its sculptors dropping a mallet on a coworker's foot. And many cul-tures have their traditions of slapstick: from Punch and Judy and clowns (one theory is that this word comes from Scandinavia—in Icelandic, *klunni*, in Swedish *kluns*, meaning clumsy person), to the Turkish Karagöz, a shadow puppet with a penchant for boast-ing and absurd violence—in one story he attempts to stop a fight by banging both parties over the head with an oversized watering can, which he ends up swinging so violently that he then knocks himself out.

In 2011, a group of evolutionary psychologists at the University of Oxford studying the relationship between laughter and our ability to withstand pain noticed a peculiar thing: people only tend to really guffaw, that *I-think-I-might-die-it-hurts-so-much* laughter, in response to slapstick. In the course of their experiments, they showed a series of short comic clips of sitcoms, stand-ups, cartoons and so on (and also, the most boring clips they could think of, which turned out to be a game of golf—sorry golfers). It was the childlike, disaster-prone Mr. Bean who caused the real gut-wobblers. For them, this was intriguing: belly laughing, which involves the lungs completely, and painfully, emptying, appears to be unique to humans, who also tend to laugh more vigorously in groups (hence, the contagion effect of canned laughter). These belly laughs create a mild euphoria that other kinds of laughter do not— and the experiment found they were capable of dulling our sensitivity to pain by up to 10 percent.

Laughing at someone else's pain might lessen our own, yet across many cultures these uninhibited belly laughs have been laden with social anxiety, and not only because they suggest a lack of compassion. Some have snobbishly regarded noisy guffawing as uncouth, linking it to uneducated lower classes incapable of self-control. In seventeenth-century Dutch painting, for instance, peasants laugh open-mouthed, displaying rotten teeth and stringy saliva, while the aristocrats remain tight-lipped. A similar connection between styles of laughing and class is found in western India in the early sixteenth century: the Sanskrit poet Bhanu Datta, in his *Rasatarangani* (River of Rasa), compares audience responses to a comic play—the upper classes snicker, the middle classes chuckle and the lower classes bellow and guffaw, tears streaming down their cheeks. In some cultures, belly laughter is not just dis-tasteful but downright dangerous: the Warlpiri of Yuendumu, in central Australia, believe the stomach is the seat of all passions, and because of this, think painful laughter at another's accidents leads to emotional upset.

There may be caution about belly laughs in some cultures, but based on their findings, the University of Oxford scientists ven-tured that this kind of laughter has been crucial to our survival. Laughing heartily at people falling over or being whacked on the head by a mallet must have its roots in our furthest prehistory, our pleasure in the mishaps of others helping us survive, allowing us to cope better with physical hardship and, more crucially, bonding us together in the groups that have protected us. And if this reac-tion is hardwired in us, how young does it start?

MERCILESS BABIES

I am sitting in a laboratory at Goldsmiths, University of London, in a small cubical draped with black curtains. There are two seats. One is for me. The other, which has a child's booster seat attached to it, is for E, my by-then nine-month-old baby. There are cameras positioned at various points on the curtains, all directed at us. And in front of us sits Dr. Caspar Addyman. Shaking a rattle.

Caspar is a developmental psychologist and founder of the Baby Laughter Project, whose aim is to understand what makes babies laugh and why. It sounds like a project of great charm and whimsy — and Caspar, with his bright-blue hair, has the air of relaxed geniality you might expect from someone whose job it is to make babies laugh all day. But to Caspar, studying the origins of laughter, its point zero, is crucial if we want to understand not only laughter itself, but how we bond with one another, learn and survive.

We try one of his experiments. E giggles as Caspar blows raspberries and I tickle him. It's all very lovely.

"Do babies experience Schadenfreude?" I ask, glancing a little nervously toward the chubby, sparkling-eyed E, who is now sitting on my knee grinning delightedly at a dinosaur sock puppet.

"Well *Freud* thought so, didn't he," Caspar says, and grimaces.

Freud has this theory in *The Joke and Its Relation to the Unconscious* that children don't really have a sense of humor. What they have instead is a taste for gloating and triumph, which emerges in those rare moments that they feel superior to the adults around them. "The child will laugh out of a feeling of superiority or *Schadenfreude*," writes Freud, "you've fallen down—I haven't." "It is the laughter of pure pleasure"—pleasure, for Freud, being the gratification of all urges, but especially the desire to overpower, or triumph over, others, and especially others who wield some power over you.

"It's horrible," says Caspar. "It's very Freud. I think it's completely wrong."

I point out that my three-year-old is always very excited to see me or her father mess up, when we mispronounce something or get confused about a friend's name. Sometimes we deliberately make mistakes, just because it brings her such joy to laugh at us. Most parents of preschool children are familiar with this (*aren't they?*). Caspar agrees that there might be pleasure, but not for the reasons Freud suggests. Children "aren't very aware of their own limitations...they're not obsessing over their failures in the way Freud assumes they're going to be."

Caspar opens his computer and shows me two graphs relating to what parents and caregivers say their babies laugh at. When asked how often the baby laughed when they themselves fell over, the overwhelming majority of parents answered "often" or "very often." When asked how often the baby laughed when someone else fell over, the answer was unanimous: "never."

This makes sense—seeing another child fall, hurt themselves and cry would be frightening for a baby, never mind if the person who hurt themselves was one of their caretakers. But to Caspar, the fact that babies don't laugh when other people fall over is about not simply fear, but morality: "Historically, everyone thought babies were amoral, and you had to teach them right from wrong, but they do have a sense of fairness and a strong sense of empathy—if someone has hurt themselves, babies can see that and are concerned."

But what about less dramatic failures? I tell Caspar a story about a friend of mine who once tried to entertain his baby by juggling, imagining the child would be delighted by all the colors and movement. The baby showed no interest whatsoever, until my friend accidentally dropped the balls, sending them bouncing across the floor, and he went scurrying after them. The baby enjoyed *that* greatly, and unleashed a peal of raspy giggles (the merciless bugger). If babies don't enjoy adults actually falling over, how about seeing them mess up once in a while?

Caspar chuckles, and tells me about the director of Theatr Iolo, Sarah Argent, who makes theater for babies and very young children. "She told me the one thing guaranteed to get all the babies laughing was when one of the performers accidentally dropped something. They really love that."

Older children do develop a taste for more serious injuries (as we'll discover in Chapter 3). But if babies aren't laughing because they feel superior, as Freud thought, then why do they find our incompetence so amusing? For Caspar, laughter is interesting because it is connected to learning, and so much of what makes babies laugh is to do with surprise: games like peekaboo or things suddenly being turned upside down help them learn about the world, their laughter—as it is with adults—a sign of seeing the world afresh.

THE UNEXPECTED

Cool Guy swings back on his chair, and it tips over.

A barman drops a tray of glasses in a busy pub.

When BBC Radio 4 Today program presenter James Naughtie accidentally introduced his next guest, then culture secretary Jeremy Hunt, as Jeremy Cunt—and then valiantly attempted to deliver the morning news bulletin amid fits of gasping giggles, at one point pretending he was having a coughing fit, which just made everyone laugh even more.

A burst water pipe sends water fifty feet into the air. The seams of a flour sack burst. An empty car, hand brake off, rolls back into a lamppost. The sociologist Roger Caillois knew all about the exciting delirium we feel witnessing destruction. He called it "Ilinx," from the Greek word for "whirlpool," and considered its disorientation akin to the euphoria created by mystical trances. As studies of vandalism have found, this pleasure is increased with an element of unpredictability. Think about Beyoncé's video for "Hold Up." She walks along the street smiling and mock swinging a baseball bat (will she, won't she?), and then suddenly smashes a car window.

The human brain requires a great deal of predictability, without which we would quickly become overwhelmed. We search for patterns and learn how to anticipate how the world will behave. So when it surprises us, with its unexpectedly high curb stones, abandoned garden rakes and manholes masquerading as puddles, we get a giddy turn. Minor accidents can be liberating and leveling. They remind us of the absurdity of living in a world which continually thwarts us. They diminish us too. The Japanese senryū poem is a comic relative of the haiku. And even in this eighteenth-century example, with its pared-back style, it is possible to detect a wicked glint of mockery at the person's vain illusion of control punctured:

> Amusingly
> Robbed of his umbrella
> In a whirlwind

In his essay "Laughter" written in 1900, Henri Bergson suggested "picture to yourself certain characters in a certain situation:

if you reverse the situation and invert the roles, you obtain a comic scene." A sudden drop in status is just such a reversal: the person who once seemed in control and dignified suddenly appears bewildered. Picture this: a presenter stands on a boat holding a giant fish while talking in a serious and grown-up way about local environmental issues. The fish, which had been quite still, suddenly starts flopping. The presenter squeals and drops it, and it flops violently all over the boat. In her fright, she attempts to jump into the arms of the angler behind her.

Our emotions can surprise us, and make us look silly (in fact, in the seventeenth and eighteenth centuries, a "surprize," as it was then spelled, meant being seized by a strong passion, as in "a Surprize of Fear"). There can be great glee, for instance, in hearing about some of the things people find themselves saying and doing when they are embarrassed. Consider this tale (as told by the English philosopher John Aubrey, author of the gossipy *Brief Lives*):

> The Earle of Oxford once bowed to Queen Elizabeth and "happened to let a Fart, at which he was so abashed and ashamed" that he went into exile for 7 years. On his returne the Queen welcomed him home, and sayd, "My Lord, I had forgott the Fart."

Or this (sent in to the BBC for a feature about horrible dates):

> Driving back after a lovely meal at a Chinese restaurant we pulled into a quiet spot on a country lane in Aldworth. Suddenly I felt my meal drop from

stomach to bowel in one lurch. I knew I couldn't hold it. I also couldn't exactly say I needed to find a toilet, so I pretended I'd been bitten on the bottom by a wasp and leapt out of the car, just managing to squat down by the rear bumper.

As I relieved myself I badly attempted to disguise the sound with sudden coughing bouts. I could hear my date asking from inside the car if I was all right whilst I scrabbled about for anything I could find to clean myself up with, all the time providing a running commentary to my date about my "bite" and insisting she stay in the car as there were more wasps.

Eventually, satisfied I'd managed to control the situation, I stood up, pulled up my jeans and sat back in the car, immediately realizing my nightmare wasn't over and was about to get worse. The back of my jeans were covered and the smell was unbearable.

As I sat in horror my date burst into fits of laughter and jumped out of the car. But her laughter was short lived. As she made her way round the back of the car to come to my aid, she stepped right into the middle of it.

We never saw each other again.

If it is amusing to see how people behave when embarrassed, what about when they are insulted? It's not so much what has been said that makes the victim's status plummet and the reversal occur, as the way insults baffle and fluster and render us speechless—and then, moments later, leave us fixated on finding the perfect response. This is, at least, what I imagine happens when people leave below-the-line comments after a divisive article in *The Guardian*. Scroll through and sooner or later, you'll find some obnoxious troll has set off a stink bomb—and then, instead of sensibly ignoring it, a handful of other commenters become so enraged that they pile on responses to the long-gone troll, their arguments getting longer and more complicated until they turn into mini-theses (some have footnotes).

Is there a point where this subsection of Schadenfreude, this sniggering at people who have got themselves wound up or are flustered by strong and unexpected emotion, tips over into sadism? What sort of person, for instance, enjoys seeing someone genuinely scared? In 2016, four people from the YouTube channel Trollstation staged a fake robbery at the National Portrait Gallery, causing panic and distress. It wasn't the first time (or the last) that vloggers have staged extreme "terror pranks"—fake bombs, or stunts that look like acid attacks—and posted them online in pursuit of clicks. When the National Portrait Gallery hoaxers were imprisoned, the judge said that part of the aim had been to "humiliate" the victims by "recording their terrified reactions to upload on the Internet." They were, one might argue, effective in this: the clip has been watched nearly a million times on YouTube. Seeing someone annoyed (at a safe distance!) might be funny—the way their arms flap and their face goes all ugly—but seeing someone in the grip of genuine fear or pain is significantly less so. So how do we know where to draw the line?

Most fail videos cut out before you can get a sense of how badly injured the person was, or else reassure you at the end that they are fine and laughing at themselves. "Man Jumps into Frozen Pool" was one of the latter. But there are other fail videos, such as "Grape Lady," which leave the camera rolling just a bit too long. "Grape Lady" is a video of a local journalist interviewing the organizer of a Grape Treading Festival in Atlanta on live TV. Both journalist and organizer have their trousers rolled up and are each standing in a barrel of grapes, pummeling the fruit with their bare feet. It's already ridiculous, but then the interviewer overbalances and tumbles off the stage. "Grape Lady" definitely made me laugh. Until, that is, I heard her frantic crying that she was in pain and had hurt her leg. She sounded vulnerable and scared. The Schadenfreude soured immediately and I felt ashamed.

"Grape Lady" has, nevertheless, been watched nearly 19 million times. "I can't understand you," wrote one person in the message board under this video. "I can't understand why anyone would find this funny," wrote another. "Is it a generation thing," wonders one. "Are you all psychopaths?!?!?!?!?!?!?!?!?!" says another.

And in between these expressions of bafflement and horror, a lone accusation: "It makes you feel powerful, doesn't it."

2

Glory
Blood, sport and triumph

When the kid who always bests you on sports day wets himself and has to go home.

When your barroom pool nemesis attempts to jump the white over another ball, and the cue slips.

When the person who grows the biggest pumpkins on the allotments is discovered buying them in Tesco.

When your perfect neighbor's perfectly groomed dog rolls in fox poo and jumps on the front seat of their car.

When your work rival, who always brags about his great taste in music, puts his iPod on shuffle at the Christmas party, and his self-recorded power ballad comes on.

Roller derby is a full-contact sport, played on roller skates by all-female amateur teams. It started in America in the 1930s, when roller skating was all the rage, and quickly took off as sports entertainment—part genuine contest, part staged. In the 2000s, it was rediscovered as a genuine sport, stripped of its staged elements and given a DIY, punk, riot grrrl makeover. Today there are over a thousand leagues worldwide. Some of the camp sports-entertainment elements have been retained. There is plenty of pre-match showboating. There are spangly, colorful leotards and leggings, and loud music and disco lights. There are face paints and pseudonyms, swagger and sass. One London team, the Rockin' Rollers, features a Pauline Foul'er, a Barbarolla and one Wiley Minogue.

It is also extremely dangerous. It involves two teams of five players skating improbably fast around an elliptical track, shoving one another out of the way to let their team's "jammer" overtake the pack. It is illegal to hit above the shoulders or below mid-thigh. But even legal hits can be pretty brutal. It is not uncommon for skaters to trip and fall sprawling onto the track or fly into the crowd. Pileups are common, as are blood, bruises and concussions.

On the night I went, "my" team was losing when the star of the opposing team fell. The crowd whistled and clapped as she was stretchered off the track, her injury an emblem of valor rather than weakness. Clutching my warm beer in a plastic cup, I joined the cheering, wanting to encourage and hail her bravery. But I'm not going to lie. Among all this camaraderie, I felt quicken in me a little pulse of expectancy, the sudden uplift of anticipation: her pain would undoubtedly mean our gain.

VILE BODIES

*When my cousin accidentally swallowed a
globule of her dentist's snot.*

*When my flatmate opened the fridge, noticed a glass of
freshly squeezed orange juice standing there, took a
gulp—and realized it was beaten egg yolks.*

*When a friend-of-a-friend's tongue swelled up and she
had to go to hospital and have it injected and
"squeezed like a giant zit."*

In the Farrelly Brothers' 1998 comedy *There's Something About
Mary*, Ted (Ben Stiller) goes to pick up Mary, his beautiful date
(Cameron Diaz), on prom night, and once there he visits the bathroom. Rushing to do up his trousers, he manages to get his scro-
tum trapped in three separate places in his zipper.

Mary's stepdad eventually barges into the bathroom, and is
aghast. Her mom comes in next and can barely look. A policeman, responding to reports of a screaming woman, pokes his head
through the window, incredulous. A firefighter arrives, and radios
his crew to come see, and to bring a camera. Finally, we actually
get to see the injury—pearly pink, glandular bulges through the
zip's sharp metal teeth. It is impossible not to recoil and squeal.

"There is the satisfaction of being able to look at the image without flinching," wrote Susan Sontag, and "there is the pleasure of flinching."

People love sharing anecdotes about horrifying physical predicaments—the more outrageous, the more awe and revulsion they provoke, the better. There is giddy surprise in bodies misbehaving, as discussed in the previous chapter. But also, surely, alongside this surprise is a little twinge of superiority. The seventeenth-century philosopher Thomas Hobbes remains influential in how we think about this link between other people's laughable failures and our own sudden rise in status. "Laughter," he wrote, "is nothing else but a sudden glory arising from sudden conception of some eminency in ourselves, by comparison with the infirmities of others." Even our own past "infirmities," compared to our present accomplishments, can provide this feeling of giddy domination, "for men laugh at the follies of themselves past."

One of the reasons Schadenfreude can seem so nasty is that this feeling of power at the expense of someone else's physical pain and clumsiness may tempt us to enjoy ever more ghoulish sights. We may shudder to think of videos of hostages being beheaded in Iraq becoming just one more piece of clickbait. But the desire to see death is an old one, and runs deep. The New York street photographer Weegee documented thousands of crime scenes in the 1930s and 1940s. Alongside the blood-spattered bodies, these images often also capture rubbernecking passersby and gawking loiterers daring themselves to peek. In 1727, John Byron, navy officer and grandfather of the poet, described in his diary strolling into town and coming across a crowd of people gathered around the sewer at Fleet Ditch, "all looking at a poor fellow that had fallen in last night or this morning, and lay dead." In *The Republic*, written in the fourth century BC, Plato describes the young nobleman Leontius wrestling with himself over his desire to gawp at the corpses of freshly executed criminals strewn outside the city walls.

Evolutionary psychologists have argued that this attraction to scenes of disaster has a purpose: ensuring we understand risks and how to avoid them. This sounds reasonable enough, but its positive spin is only part of the story. Many poets and novelists have described the feelings of mastery and domination that come with the sight of other people suffering. The novelist Charles Maturin, for instance, in his 1820 Gothic fantasy *Melmoth the Wanderer*, wrote:

> I have heard of men who have traveled into countries where horrible executions were to be daily witnessed for the sake of that excitement which the sight of suffering never fails to give…a triumph over those whose sufferings have placed them below us, and no wonder—suffering is always an indication of weakness—we glory in our impenetrability.

For almost two thousand years, much of this feeling of glory was thought to come from the contrast that's produced when we compare the miseries of the person suffering with our own better luck. One of the oldest surviving depictions of Schadenfreude appears in the Roman philosopher-poet Lucretius's *De rerum natura* (or *The Nature of Things*), written at some point between 100 BC and 50 BC. The poem itself is not very promising: there are no vindictive gods, no one accidentally has sex with their mother—it is about physics. But in the second section ("The Dance of Atoms"), Lucretius describes how philosophers, like him, serenely liberated from worldly concerns, enjoy seeing non-philosophers in a twist about money and sex (you might be pleased to know that Lucretius is rumored to have died in a frenzy of lust after accidentally swallowing a love potion). Lucretius compares his smug philosophical pleasure to that of seeing a ship in danger at sea:

> How sweet it is to watch from dry land when the
> storm-winds roil
> A mighty ocean's waters, and see another's bitter toil—
> Not because you relish someone else's misery—
> Rather, it's sweet to know from what misfortunes
> you are free.

It is hard to imagine anyone standing on the quayside enjoying the sight of a ship in peril, and yet Lucretius's image did resonate through the ages, and in cultures more reliant on sea travel than our own. As we have already seen, Hobbes spoke of watching ships being buffeted in a storm: "There must be joy in this sight" he wrote, "else men would never flock to such a spectacle." Johann Joachim Ewald's poem *The Storm* (1755) acknowledges this pleasure in his dramatic depiction of a ship caught in a gale, the sky's sudden darkness, the howling wind, the sails washed by the water: "The ship is shattered, and I... nothing happened to me, / Because I only watched the storm from shore." For Edmund Burke, the vast and roiling sea gave a feeling of "delightful horror"; to see others in peril gave the eighteenth-century art theorist Jean-Baptiste Dubos a zest for life, and kept the dreaded *ennui* at bay. The closest I have ever come is looking at Turner's 1803 painting *Calais Pier*, in which the sailors' gritty determination and wind-whipped clothes made me feel warm and snug, and faintly relieved.

In the mid-nineteenth century, however, a new explanation for this strange attraction to the sight of other people in danger emerged. As a result of Darwin's theory of evolution by natural selection, many came to believe our excitement at scenes of death and destruction were a vestige lingering from our more violent pasts. "If evolution and the survival of the fittest be true at all," wrote the psychologist William James in 1890, "the destruction of prey and human rivals *must* have been among the most important of man's primitive functions, the fighting and the chasing instincts *must* have become ingrained," and so inflicting violence or seeing an enemy mangled or destroyed would have become "intensely pleasurable." And for James, and others, organized sports were the archetypal modern expression of this ancient violence. "See the ignoble crew that escorts every great pugilist—parasites who feel as if the glory of his brutality rubbed off upon them... [they] share the rapture without enduring the pains!" Somewhere, in the oldest and most easily confused parts of our brains, we feel they suffer *because* we have beaten them, their subjugation *is* our triumph.

TRIUMPH

When, at the critical moment of the Olympics Dressage, another country's horse poops.

When your favorite figure-skater's nemesis trips.

When Brazil was knocked out of the World Cup in a shocking defeat, Americans were really pleased and went crazy posting pictures—first of excited, dressed-up, reveling Brazilians, then of disbelieving and tense-looking Brazilians, and finally of weeping Brazilians, with captions such as "So, Brazil had kind of a rough day" or "Want a hug?"

Is it possible to imagine sport without Schadenfreude? The bungled shot that skewers a rival, the fumbled ball that leads us to triumph? Mistakes, as William Carlos Williams, writing about the crowds at a baseball game, well knew, are part of the drama of the game: "the chase / and the escape, the error / the flash of genius." The players themselves must be gracious, of course (though I have it on good authority that when their opponent hits the ball into the rough, golfers feel a secret clutch of triumph that they'd never, *never* admit; "golf is a game for hypocrites," one told me).

This same etiquette rarely constrains the fans. Since its first appearance in the eleventh century, the word *sport* has been associated with mockery and ridicule (as in: "to make sport of someone"). Our own team's mistakes may exasperate us, but those of the other side earn our most triumphant contempt. In some sports crowing at unforced errors is exceedingly bad manners. The Wimbledon rules outlaw flash photography, selfie sticks and Schadenfreude: "Never applaud a net cord or double fault." *Never!* Of course, sometimes things get out of hand. When British hopeful Heather Watson faced world no. 1 Serena Williams on Centre Court in 2015, the home crowd, unable to restrain themselves a moment longer, let out a strangled cheer of delight at Williams's unforced faults, forcing her to remonstrate with the umpire. And we all know the kind of parent who, when his nine-year-old's gymnastics nemesis lands awkwardly from her backflip, clenches his fist and hisses "Yes!"

You might think that a rival's mistake is especially pleasurable when we stand to win as a result. In fact, many studies of sports fans have shown that our own success is not half so enjoyable as our bitter rival's failure. Remember the study of the sports fans who smiled more broadly when their rivals missed a penalty than when their team scored? This is certainly not the only time this phenomenon has been observed. During the 2010 World Cup, two Dutch psychologists, Jaap W. Ouwerkerk and Wilco W. van Dijk, both avid football fans, developed a grubby habit. With the Dutch team still in the tournament, the pair watched the games on a Dutch channel, switching over to a foreign broadcaster when the Dutch team did particularly well, for the gratification of hearing another commentator's praise. As soon as the Dutch team was knocked out, the psychologists started paying close attention to their bitter longtime rivals, the Germans. In the semifinal, Spain scored the winning goal against Germany minutes before the whistle blew. The psychologists excitedly grabbed their remote controls and switched over to the German channel ADR — just so they could sit back and relish the satisfaction of hearing the German commentators forced to describe their own imminent defeat. They were not the only ones. They later discovered that the number of Dutch people watching the match on the German broadcaster had peaked at 352,000 just before the end of the match, when it was clear that the Germans would be defeated; a media analyst dubbed this "Schadenfreude density."

Why would a rival's defeat bring such happiness, even if it does not mean we are any more likely to win ourselves? Perhaps we think of the long game, and hope our rival's confidence will be shaken. Perhaps we will view it as payback for some earlier humiliating defeat of our own. As will be discussed further in Chapter 8, when we humans organize ourselves into rival tribes, the competitiveness that emerges is far stronger than any seen between individuals. One of its effects is that the more identified we are with our own tribe, the more inclined we are to see a rival as a two-dimensional representative of the other side, rather than a fully formed human. This is not a comfortable thought for many reasons — and its influence can be felt in far more serious arenas than sport. But it might go some way to explaining that rather unpleasant and furtive form of Schadenfreude sometimes experienced by sports fans: the involuntary stab of happiness felt when another team's top player is injured.

When in 2008 the New England Patriots' star quarterback Tom Brady fell badly after a hit from a player for the Kansas City Chiefs, his scream stunned Gillette Stadium into silence. There was, however, no stunned silence in the bars and living rooms in New York: when Brady fell, reported a *New York Times* editor who had been watching the NFL game in a Midtown Manhattan bar, "people in the restaurant roared with delight." And when it turned out that Brady's injury was a torn ligament, serious enough to force him to sit out the season, Internet chat rooms went mad with excitement.

It wasn't to everyone's taste. "Cheering when a player is injured is the epitome of classlessness," wrote one commentor on the *New York Times*' Fifth Down blog. "To actually stand up and cheer when a fellow human being has suffered a painful injury? There is something very wrong there. Don't give me this BS about honesty and 'expressing your feelings,' there are some lines that should not be crossed." Others were more pragmatic: "to see Brady out of the season will make beating the Pats meaningless... Sport is made great by the best facing the best."

But the main thing I noticed as I scrolled through these comments is how often people defended their Schadenfreude by saying that the player *deserved it*. The fans who cheered were rapturous— as James had put it—euphoric at the possibility of their win. But when asked, they defended this pleasure with the most apparently rational of reasons. The Pats deserved it. They deserved it for cheating. They deserved it for some previous underhand tackle. They deserved it for historical grievances. Most of all, they deserved it for being smug.

"You better believe I'd have joined in," wrote one commentor who took to his keyboard with an exultant air. "I cheered in the comfort of my own vehicle. That smug schmuck and his cheating coach deserve some comeuppance... Yeah, I'm bitter. It's the story of any Raiders fan's life."

3

Justice

Karma and compulsion

A stranger tweets: "Send prayers & good wishes for the guy who tried to pick my pocket, took out a tampon, got mortified & tried to put it back."

When someone jumps the queue for the cash machine and then the machine swallows their card.

When a married Ohio legislator, who vociferously campaigned against LGBTQ rights, resigns after he is reportedly discovered in his office having sex with a man.

The other day, I was on a train when an email pinged into my phone. It was from my husband. "Have you seen this?!?!" was the subject line.

When I was in my twenties and worked as a theater director, I once had a more senior male colleague who endlessly flirted with the female playwrights and actresses we worked with, sleazily rating their attractiveness behind their backs. I didn't stay long at that particular theater for a number of reasons, but this was among them.

After the Harvey Weinstein allegations surfaced in Hollywood, and social media erupted with the #MeToo campaign, I happened to read an interview with this now-influential director, in which he said this: "I think the search for who is the Weinstein of British theater is an honorable search and some names have come up. More may come up. It is a terribly traumatic process and it's right that we are examining it and bringing stuff to light." I was incredulous. Did he not *realize*?

The email from my husband arrived a few weeks after this. It was a link to a news story. After reading that same interview, five women had come forward alleging cases of historic harassment against the director.

Let me be clear: I do not know the details of the allegations. But I also have to admit that the experience of the women involved was not at the forefront of my mind in that exact moment. What I felt — and it is hard to describe this precisely — was a kind of ecstasy, as if a clean white light had exploded inside me. I could not stop grinning.

POETRY

*The man insulting the airport check-in staff discovers
he has forgotten his passport.*

*The driver who nicked your parking spot is still, five
minutes later, attempting to maneuver back and forth
into it, while you saunter past into the shop.*

*The colleague who keeps heating fish in the
microwave, and stinks out the whole open-plan
office, gets food poisoning.*

Nothing makes the world gleam like bad people getting the fate they deserve. For one glorious moment, the stars align, the universe delivers and the commuter who barged past us down the station stairs, knocking the shopping out of our hands, misses their train. As we glide onto the platform, we watch as they curse and check their watch and curse again, and feel ourselves warmed with self-satisfaction. *Karma*, we think smugly. *What goes around comes around.* No wonder we crane round to catch a glimpse of the fare dodger caught, or the face of the car driver who has been pulled over: little is more pleasing than seeing a transgressor get their comeuppance.

Søren Kierkegaard called the pleasure in another's downfall

"loathsome." Charles Baudelaire wrote: "what clearer sign of debility could there be than a nervous convulsion, an involuntary spasm, comparable to a sneeze, caused by the sight of another's misfortune?" But most writers in history have agreed that there is one situation in which we may well be entitled to enjoy the spectacle of someone else's misery, and that is *when they deserve it*.

The eighteenth-century German philosopher Immanuel Kant, for instance, believed humans were naturally predisposed to "fellow feeling," or what we would call "empathy." Yet watching the behavior of other Germans at the time taught him something that cold, hard logic could not: "When someone who delights in annoying and vexing peace-loving folk receives at last a right good beating, it is certainly an ill but everyone approves of it and considers it a good in itself." Kant concluded that the pleasure we take in punishment is not malicious, but stems from the relief of seeing moral equilibrium restored. Even the criminal himself, he wrote, perhaps a little optimistically, would celebrate his punishment.

One of the stories we tell ourselves about modern Western justice is that it is unemotional and sober. Long gone are the whipping posts and stocks of Kant's world. Instead of crowds rushing to the gallows to jeer and whoop, in the UK at least, official, state-sanctioned punishment largely happens behind closed doors. When we think of justice today, dispassionate judges and rational deliberation are the ideals that spring to mind.

Yet justice is also hugely emotional. When in 2009 the swindler Bernard Madoff received his 150-year prison sentence, the public gallery erupted in cheers and applause. A murderer is imprisoned and the tabloids print stock pictures of prison cells and uniforms, salivating over their unpleasantness. Plenty of TV shows turn on "Gotcha!" moments in which criminals are caught—they range from the suburban nightmare of *Cowboy Builders* to the deeply suspect *To Catch a Predator* (in which older men contact "under-age girls" online, arrange to meet, and are instead greeted by TV cameras and police—as one online commenter put it: "He peed himself, LOL"). And it is impossible to miss the rapid fire of moral condemnation online ricocheting around our echo chambers, and which we celebrate with likes and shares. These moments of high emotion are intriguing because they break through the social veneer. Are we *allowed* to gloat? Are we entitled to add an extra dose of humiliation to the carefully measured punishment? In these moments of curdled pleasure and shame, we might wonder not just why we feel so good, but how far we would be willing to go to get that hit.

JUSTICE JUNKIES

When a grown man on a microscooter whizzes past a group of elderly people on the zebra crossing and then hits the curb.

When a disciplinarian childcare guru's own kids are caught having a meltdown in the supermarket.

Schadenfreude

When your flatmate chucked your washing out of the machine to put hers in — and then left a red sock in with her whites.

In high school, James Kimmel Jr. was bullied by a group of other boys. It was a sustained campaign of abuse, over many years, culminating in them shooting and killing Jim's dog. The police did nothing. One night when he was alone at the family home, the bullies arrived and let off a small bomb inside the postbox before driving away. "I snapped," he tells me over the phone from his office at the Yale School of Medicine, where he now works. He grabbed a loaded gun — he lived on a farm — got in his car and went after them.

Jim followed them through the darkness to their farm. When they stopped, Jim stopped too, and, dazzling them with his headlights, he began getting out of his car holding the loaded gun. And in that moment, he says, he had a kind of revelation. "I realized that if I murdered them I would be murdering myself. It was just enough to see that it would be a horrific price to pay." So he pulled the door shut and drove home again. And he started planning to become a lawyer.

The trauma of that high school experience never left Jim, and his legal career was not quite the happy ending he expected. "I was drawn to litigation. I listened to my clients' tales of injustice and empathized with them, as you must do as a lawyer, and this tapped a powerful desire to see justice done within me." A decade of this work brought Jim to a breaking point. "I sought justice everywhere in every way I could...at the grocery store, when someone cut me off in traffic, I wanted to inflict that pain back...it started to feel extremely dysfunctional." Eventually he was forced to wind down his legal practice.

And then he happened to open the *New York Times*, and read a story about one of the first brain-imaging experiments that looked at the pleasure of justice. The study, carried out by Swiss researchers in 2004, claimed that people are so motivated by the pleasure of seeing justice done that, while playing gambling games, they are willing to pay money to see cheats and freeloaders punished. The researchers linked this to activation of the dorsal striatum, an area of the brain implicated in the processing of rewards, including the pleasure of taking narcotics. If the pleasure of punishing others was enough to make you spend money, Jim wondered, was it enough to get you addicted?

It is no surprise that justice feels good. Cooperation and rules are vital for keeping our societies harmonious and predictable—punishing those who transgress and are untrustworthy even more so (during experiments like the one described above, when participants are not allowed to punish transgressors, the game quickly breaks down). A more recent study has suggested that this desire to punish exists whether or not the person realizes or might learn from the experience (as when the waiter spits in the rude customer's soup). Even children as young as six years old enjoy watching selfish or untrustworthy figures punished (and, in case you were wondering, feel empathetic distress when someone who has been generous to them suffers).

A group of researchers in Leipzig set up a puppet theater where some puppets were nice and friendly and others behaved unkindly to the children; for example, by proffering a favorite toy and then snatching it away again. The puppets were then individually punished by being hit. Seeing the good puppets beaten upset the children. But when it came to the bad ones, they were positively gleeful. It gets worse. The children were allowed to see a quick burst of punishment, before the puppet theater curtains were drawn shut. But if the children wanted to keep watching the punishment, they had to pay with tokens. And when it came to the selfish puppets, the children paid.

In ordinary life, we often incur a cost to tell someone off—risking social embarrassment, and worse, physical retaliation. The pleasurable reward we receive to compensate is clearly very strong. So could we really become addicted to justice? Jim Kimmel certainly thinks so, and has dedicated himself to raising awareness of its risks, moving from life as a justice-craving lawyer to a psychiatry lecturer and researcher. He points to a study that suggests differences in processing dopamine may cause some of us to be genetically disposed to enjoy justice more than others, and another that shows that men apparently tend to derive more pleasure than women from seeing wrongdoers punished.

There is even a study that suggests that pleasure peaks at the point when we anticipate a punishment (for those children, the moment just after they pay and before the puppet-theater curtains open again) but drops off dramatically afterward, since getting even usually involves the reopening of old wounds. And this is true whether we are enacting the punishment ourselves or simply watching it from the sidelines. Kimmel believes that the risks of justice addiction are huge: terrorism, vengeful murders, gang crimes. But even at the more minor end of the spectrum, most of us crave the satisfaction of getting even. Perhaps we're already hooked.

If ever there was an environment that would leave us jonesing for a next hit of justice, it is the digital world. Along with fail videos, Twitter pile-ons and Facebook rants at moral slights are often held up as evidence that we are living in an Age of Schadenfreude, especially eager for spiteful retaliations from the comfort of our living room couches. The Schadenfreude we express seeing a rule-breaker shamed can be a force for good and transform public conversations (about which, see Chapter 8). But just as often its special brand of mob justice can be catastrophic—and unnervingly easy to succumb to.

Social media platforms may argue that they are neutral, but it is becoming clear how profoundly they shape our sense of injustice. It is likely that we are exposed to far more misdeeds online than in our face-to-face interactions, when breaking news stories of genocides, corrupt bankers and international conspiracies ping up in the corner of our screens. Revenue-driven algorithms that promote the most shareable content—the more outrage-provoking it is, the more it seems we click—makes this situation more febrile. But perhaps what makes online moral indignation so compulsive is that it comes with almost no effort or cost. Hiding behind our screens, we do not have to face up to transgressors in the flesh, to risk a punch or social humiliation in the real world. And, since studies show we are more likely to punish when others are watching, we already have an audience. If we want to derive pleasure from seeing people get their comeuppance, hanging around online is the easiest way to do it.

Remember Justine Sacco? She made a catastrophic error of judgment and tweeted this—clumsy, tin-eared—joke about racial privilege to her 170 followers: *Going to Africa. Hope I don't get AIDS. Just kidding. I'm white!* By the time she got off the plane, her phone had exploded with the full righteous fury of the Internet. When the British writer Jon Ronson—who subsequently interviewed Sacco about the life-changing evisceration she received as a result—first saw the fallout on Twitter, his first response, he admits, was this: "an initial happy little 'Oh, wow, someone is *fucked.*'"

AWKWARDNESS

The cultural theorist Adam Kotsko identifies awkwardness as a very contemporary predicament, which arises when conflicting value systems are at work and we are unsure how to behave or what to do. Schadenfreude is loaded with potential for awkwardness, especially online, where it is possible to be roused quickly to moral outrage, and just as quickly to find ourselves changing our minds in the face of just a little more information. The neuroscientist Sophie Scott, who studies laughter, for instance, notes that young people always chortle during her lectures when she shows a video clip of a Dublin pedestrian slipping on ice. But elderly people, who are themselves more likely to slip on ice, rarely laugh, no doubt embarrassing the younger people into an awkward silence. It is a situation aptly summed up by a headline in the satirical paper *The Onion*: "That's not funny; my brother died that way."

Such missteps remind us that our perception of suffering as deserved—and our willingness to gloat over a punishment—can change very quickly indeed. The line between what is fair suffering and what is unfair suffering moves around a lot, and is often not universally agreed on. And so this raises the question: How do we decide what others deserve?

Lisa Feldman Barrett, neuroscientist and author of *How Emotions are Made*, usually gets disqualified from jury duty when they find out what she does for a living. Why? I ask. Because of this sort of thing, she grins. She had recently done a stint of jury duty. "I was appalled, actually. Everything I worry about as a scientist actually did happen." It had been a civil case, a man suing a gas station for negligence after slipping and falling in a spill. The jury denied him compensation, and Lisa felt waves of quiet satisfaction envelop the jury room as they reached their decision, 6–1. Lisa, as you've probably already guessed, was the odd one out.

The problem was their brains. Brains, as Lisa puts it, "are very expensive organs to run," and so they are very good at predicting things and sorting things into predefined categories, to reduce effort and free up energy for other tasks. "We think what we are seeing is objectively true, but actually we are constantly curating our experience to fit in with what we already know." When it comes to finding someone innocent or guilty this confirmation bias is a particular risk.

The plaintiff was not from the U.S. originally, and was not a native English speaker. "There was an anti-immigrant kind of a focus in the discussions. If you had in mind the idea that there were immigrants who were trying to put one over on the government, or on your American gas station brand…" She pauses. "I wouldn't go so far as to say delight, but there was a sense of satisfaction about having stopped someone taking advantage of the system."

For Lisa, the fact that we feel any satisfaction at all at another's comeuppance is extraordinary. "The brain can't take in all the information around it, so it makes decisions on what seems relevant," putting information which might impact us directly into what Lisa calls our own "affective niche." It is obvious enough that if someone approaches you with a knife, you will interpret that as pertinent information, and experience strong and metabolically costly emotions as a result. But the fact that we can feel a powerful sensation—whether laughter or white-hot vindication—when someone is being punished, even when we are neither the victim nor responsible for enacting the punishment, suggests that our brains find this kind of scenario just as significant. "It is amazing that my brain is responding to something as relevant to me and my body that isn't happening to me at all, that's happening very far away, that I might never actually see with my own eyes."

The reason we care is undoubtedly that on some level we feel that what endangers other people might also threaten us. "Do I feel the same Schadenfreude about the capture of a villain who has harmed a man as a villain who harms a woman? Do I feel the same degree of Schadenfreude toward a person who harms a child before or after I have children?" she wonders. It seems unlikely, given how much evidence there is showing that we empathize more strongly with those who are similar to us, while feeling a less urgent pain at the suffering of those we categorize as "other." The hackles of our moral indignation rise most forcefully when the transgression could affect us.

Why else would I, a committed pedestrian (I can't drive), feel such satisfaction when people who cycle on pavements are pulled over by the police? Or when I read a satirical article that claims students who leave negative feedback about their university lecturers (I am one of these lecturers) are shown to be bad in bed? Or when people who make TV programs about the glories of a pristine house are discovered to live in total squalor (like me)?

Along with a hatred of rule breakers and hypocrites, part of what motivates my pleasure to see others brought to justice is self-defense. Their transgressions might affect me in the future. And so I revel in the spectacle of their comeuppance in the hope that they will be forced to learn from it, and amend the errors of their ways.

4

The Smug

Superiority, pretensions and fantasy comeuppances

When the state-of-the-art glass walls at Apple's new Norman Foster–designed HQ, Apple Park campus, achieve such high levels of transparency that workers are injured walking into them, and resort to sticking Post-it Notes on the glass so people know it's there.

When the doorbell rings and I find my husband, who regularly gives me tutorials on correct key management, has forgotten his keys.

While watching a video of parents smugly showing off their new Echo Dot by getting their toddler to request a song. Toddler: "Play Digger Digger." Alexa: "You want to hear a station for porn, hot chick amateur girl? Pussy, anal, dildo." Parents (in background): "No! Alexa! Stop! Stop!" ("Digger Digger" also appears to be the name of a porn video.)

About six months ago, I went to the National Gallery. It was autumn and the tourists had gone. The gallery was quiet, and I happened to drift past a painting by Pieter Bruegel the Elder, painted around 1555. Unusually for me, I read the title card first—*Landscape with the Fall of Icarus*—and I looked briefly at the canvas for the man who, lusting for fame and glory, tried to fly to the sun. I expected to see a muscular hero in giant prosthetic wings crashing to earth in a ball of flames; no, it was a quiet-looking cliff-edge view. I checked the title again: *Landscape with the Fall of Icarus*. Looked back—nope. Here was a bucolic scene of a farmer tending his sheep, of clouds scudding and scrubby grass growing and a boat rocking in a quiet bay. And then I spotted him. In the bottom right hand of the painting, unseen by any of the farmers or sheep, or viewers, having plopped into the water head first, merely a pair of tiny upside-down flailing legs. There aren't many paintings in the National Gallery which make me laugh, but this does. Icarus hoped to win admiration. Instead, his death goes unnoticed.

Is anything more aggravating than other people's smugness? Those wisps of moral superiority, that arrogance mixed with a little pinch of studied humility, the smothering, solicitous smile: "Well of course we did get a Prius"; "I confess, I do like to wake at sunrise to meditate." "You're forgiven," say the smug in their most patronizing voice when you apologize after a row (everyone knows the rule is *both* people have to apologize *to each other*). "You're welcome," they declaim after your muttered thanks for their (frankly, inconsequential) favor. Smugness—along with its close relatives: showing off, superiority, excessive ambition and pretentiousness— isn't precisely a crime, at least not of the same magnitude as those transgressions discussed in the previous chapter. But it does often feel like one. From Icarus to Elon Musk, hubris is the flaw we are most excited to see punished. It is a special kind of Schadenfreude, akin to that of seeing justice restored, but rather more open to abuse, since vanity and conceitedness in other people—like most of their personality flaws—is firmly in the eye of the beholder.

The Danish author Aksel Sandemose was not, by all accounts, a very likable character: he ripped off his publishers, abandoned his wife and children, and may or may not have killed a man. His work is not read that widely today, except one page of his 1933 novel *A Fugitive Crosses His Tracks*. Set in a fictional town called Jante that is much like the small North Jutland town Sandemose grew up in, the novel is famous among Danes for encapsulating their country's tacit disdain for all kinds of individualism and ambitiousness in its Rule of Jante (or *Janteloven*):

> You're not to think you *are* anything special.
> You're not to think you are as good as *we* are.
> You're not to think you are smarter than *we* are.
> You're not to imagine yourself better than *us*.
> You're not to think you know more than *we* do.
> You're not to think you are more important than
> *we* are.
> You're not to think *you* are good at anything.
> You're not to laugh at *us*.
> You're not to think anyone cares about *you*.
> You're not to think you can teach *us* anything.

And the Danish are not alone. People have sniggered with contempt at those who break these unspoken rules in many times and places. Especially when it comes to dancing. Castiglione's sixteenth-century etiquette manual, *The Book of the Courtier*, contains an anecdote about a soldier at a court party who refuses to join in with the dancing, since he is a military man and above such nonsense. A fellow guest, a woman, starts mocking him for his pretentiousness; soon there is "much laughinge of the standers by," leaving the poor soldier humiliated. Among the Torres Strait Islanders, one of Australia's indigenous communities, male dances are a central part of communal life, and their choreography is highly prescribed. So if someone attempts to show off or embellish the moves with a little extra flourish of their own? Well, the unnerving sound of women laughing at them from the shadows will quickly set them right.

In theory, in the modern West, we have shaken ourselves free of this stifling contempt for individual flair. Don't we celebrate ambition? Applaud aspiration? But you don't have to scratch the surface hard to find something like the Rule of Jante alive and well. In 2017, an "Instagram influencer" promoted a luxury music festival in the Bahamas—one of the most expensive weekend packages cost $30,000 per person—which the organizers promised would be the event of a lifetime. The bands didn't show, the white-sand beach was a building site, the food was sandwiches in plastic wrappers (and yes, it rained). How we gloated.

Truth told, we like to cut our fellow humans down to size in many small ways. My neighbor is ribbed by another neighbor for his sleek new car ("you look like an Uber driver!"). "OooOOOooo," my friends all sing in a little glissando of mock awe when one of us lets slip she's going to Harrods for brunch. There is something *de trop* about excess, and we know the rules: don't name-drop, don't boast about your kids' achievements, don't draw attention to your expensive new coat. In fact, we must know the rules, otherwise we wouldn't go to such ingenious lengths to find ways round them (cf. the humblebrag).

The dislike of those who *think they are better than the rest of us* also lies at the heart of the itch to see experts proved wrong. There is great glee in imagining big-league professionals regretting their hasty pronouncements, as when Decca Records execs rejected the Beatles in 1962, with a dismissive "Guitar groups are on the way out," or when IBM chairman Thomas Watson declared in 1943, "I think there is a world market for maybe five computers." And British people, who enjoy anything relating to the weather as much as they hate authority, still snigger about the time when, in 1987, weatherman Michael Fish laughed incredulously at a woman who had phoned the BBC to say a hurricane was on the way. "Don't worry, there isn't," he smirked. Before the greatest storm for three centuries battered the country.

Most know the idea of "tall poppies" as a shorthand for our eagerness to see outstanding and highly skilled people tripped up. There is, we suspect, an undertow of cruelty—and we'd be right. The expression originates with a story told by the Greek historian Herodotus in which the tyrant Periander, struggling to control the unruly citizens of Corinth, sought the advice of a neighboring tyrant. The advice came with a wordless gesture: the neighboring king walked through a field of wheat, silently picking off the tallest, most luscious ears until he had entirely destroyed the best part of the crop (the poppies were only swapped in to the fable later). With this Periander knew what to do, wrote Herodotus, and immediately slaughtered all notable and influential people in his city, so that he might rule unchallenged.

Is our dislike of success similarly paranoid and power-crazed? It is certainly hypocritical. We are all guilty of small vanities, moments when we want to be noticed or stand out. And yet we enjoy nothing more than waiting eagerly for other people's soufflés to deflate. Perhaps it is little more than a desire to feel better about ourselves, to go about our day unchallenged. No doubt, envy plays its part, along with our desire not to be left behind (as we'll discover more in the next chapter). When we expose such feelings in ourselves, we might also find ourselves feeling a little clammy, and suspect that we are no better than the penny-pinching Mrs. Hackit of George Eliot's story "The Sad Fortunes of the Reverend Amos Barton," with her love of mean gossip and "utmost enjoyment of spoiling a friend's self-satisfaction." Perhaps you are feeling a little ashamed right now.

As with all our vices, a suspicion of the ostentatious and outwardly successful—those tall poppies—is normal. Evolutionary psychologists have ventured that early societies, so reliant on cooperation, must have also been highly egalitarian, even if in practice these societies were not peaceful utopias, but were reliant on aggression and violence. Ridiculing and ostracizing those who domineered or tried to appear more important and deserving than the rest was one way of holding people to account. Whether in twenty-first-century London, in a sixteenth-century Venetian court or among the Torres Strait Islanders, ridiculing pretensions may seem cruel, but it also serves a communal purpose, preventing offenders from setting themselves apart from those who will protect them. *It's for your own good*, we might think. If you want to stay in our gang, you have to keep to the rules.

Today we may find ourselves trapped between two different impulses: one to celebrate individuality and flair, and the other to condemn it. But we must acknowledge the pleasures in the latter. We might ultimately be left feeling uncomfortable for sniggering inwardly when the pretentious flounder, but in that little surge of superiority, there might even be a glimmer of hope — that by taking pleasure in their downfall, we are saving them from themselves.

"GOOD SCHADENFREUDE"

"I think there is such a thing as Good Schadenfreude," the philosopher John Portmann tells me from his office at the University of Virginia. He measures his words precisely; he is — as you'd expect — extremely thoughtful and reflective. In our Age of Schadenfreude we find ourselves in an extraordinary moral dilemma, enticed to feel it and condemned when we do. With his book *When Bad Things Happen to Other People* (2000), Portmann aimed to "dispel anxiety" for those of us troubled by this unwanted feeling, a desire to console which seems to me unusually generous for an academic philosopher, who usually want to disturb and agitate.

"I'm really just a product of my background," he tells me. "I grew up in a strict Catholic home. In many religious homes, certainly mine, you're taught certain rules, and you're made to feel very guilty for failing to live up to them...I had a mother who loved me but she would say when I was growing up that I was arrogant and that this was sinful. She seemed to take some pleasure in my failures or humiliations, and she felt this was God's way of trying to teach me something or show me something. Nowadays, mothers, at least in America, are quite different...no matter what their child does they say it's absolutely brilliant. My mother was really quite strict...and um"—he takes a long pause before continuing—"and yeah so, I was very, very aware early on that sometimes when you fail you make other people quite happy."

His voice trails off. We've only been talking for a few minutes, and this revelation fills me with genuine sorrow. Yet for John this story isn't so much about misery as about how he translated this early experience into understanding how sometimes pleasure felt at another's failures can involve a longing for moral transformation—the "Good Schadenfreude" he espouses.

John tells me about a recent visit to the extraordinary baroque château Vaux-le-Vicomte, southeast of Paris. On a table, as part of a historical reconstruction, sat an early edition of the fables of seventeenth-century poet Jean de La Fontaine. It lay open at two pages of "The Lion Becomes Old." The lion had terrorized the jungle with his power and might, treating the other creatures with contempt. Everyone feared and resented him. But eventually he aged, "laden with years, and lingering away / Mourning the memory of his strength now flown / Attacked at last by subjects of his own." The animals circle around him as he lies dying, kicking, biting and mocking him. It sounds phenomenally cruel to modern ears.

But how different is it really from the Schadenfreude that accompanied, say, Jeffrey Archer's fall from grace, or Martha Stewart's—the journalists all piling in to kick them when they were down, just as the animals did to the lion? La Fontaine's cautionary tale is not so much about getting revenge for a transgression as the pleasure we feel when someone who has made us feel inferior is destroyed. Picture that kid at school—there will have been one—who was really gifted, academic and popular, sporty and confident, and who then sailed off to Oxford or Harvard and made you feel pale in comparison. Things go really well for them for a while. But a few years later you hear that their life has taken a turn, that they are now unemployed or addicted or living back at home. How do you feel?

"Life is full of ups and downs," says John, "and people do rejoice in the fact that you've lost your fangs, your claws, your power, and they remember what it felt like to be intimidated by you, and they do feel pleasure, I think."

The Christian tradition in which John was raised is highly conflicted about Schadenfreude. "Do not gloat when your enemy falls; when they stumble, do not let your heart rejoice," instructs the Old Testament (Proverbs 24:17). And yet, Christian art and literature is stuffed full of scenes which relish the suffering of sinners. Hieronymus Bosch's *The Last Judgment* is shamelessly gleeful in its vision of drunkards being forced to drink great barrels of wine, and demons wielding sharp-spiked torture machines. Tertullian, a Christian convert who lived during the second and third century AD, appears to have been positively thrilled by what might happen to his former friends come Judgment Day: the heathen poets would be "covered in shame...as one fire consumes them!"; the actors would howl more loudly than they ever had in the amphitheater; wrestlers would leap and tumble not in the gymnasia but "in the fiery billows." On earth, Schadenfreude may have been unacceptable; but when it came to the afterlife, the gloves were off.

Bosch and Tertullian's Schadenfreude involves retributive justice — a retrospective punishment for sinning (and since they take place in hell, there is no hope of redemption). But the Bible does also talk about another sort of Schadenfreude — enjoying the sight of suffering since it may lead to transformation. "I take no pleasure in the death of the wicked man, but rather in the wicked man's conversion, that he may live," says God in the Old Testament Book of Ezekiel (33:11). Public humiliation has long been part of religious discipline. The Byzantine hermits usually frowned on laughter and jokes, thinking them signs of lustfulness and cruelty (after all, Christ never laughed in the Bible). Yet the saint Athanasios of Athos, who lived in the tenth century AD, dealt with an impudent monk by encouraging his brethren to ridicule him. In early modern Christian Europe, ritualized public humiliations, including fasting, whipping and processing around churches, aimed to bring the rule breakers down to the earth (the *humus* in Latin), in the hope that they would emerge more God-fearing and respectful, and set an example to others. As recently as the mid-nineteenth century, Abraham Lincoln decreed that 30 April each year should be a "day of national humiliation," of fasting and deprivation. America, he argued, had become "intoxicated with unbroken success... too self-sufficient... too proud."

The vogue for reclaiming *our own* failures and celebrating them as part of success is a modern take on this—all of the humbling, a little less of the humiliation, since we control the narrative ourselves. Such stories can be tremendously inspiring: J. K. Rowling, for example, has spoken of the importance of becoming "the biggest failure I knew"—a lone parent, jobless, broke—to commit to what she truly cared about. Perhaps this instinct that failure helps is also part of what drives, along with our love of surprises and reversals, our taste for Internet fail videos. Take the hero of my current favorite YouTube video. A fat, gorgeous toddler and pretty fluffy kitten sit opposite each other. The toddler reaches out—we think to stroke the kitten—and punches it on the nose. The kitten rears up and swipes at the toddler with its paw. The astonished toddler falls over and starts howling. If you found this funny, you may, in fact, be celebrating the toddler learning an Important Life Lesson, from which he will emerge chastened and humbled.

Of course, we must be wary. Telling someone to their face that being dumped will "strengthen their character," or that losing a job will be "the grit that makes the pearl" is barbed at best, smuggling on board a little criticism, the implication that they have a flaw that needs correcting, and so adding insult to injury. Yes, there can be superciliousness in "Good Schadenfreude." And, when it comes to enjoying the redemption of those who have wronged us, there can also be more than a little self-delusion.

FANTASY COMEUPPANCES

*That you'll take your new rich, handsome actor/model
boyfriend to your ex's engagement party.*

*That your immaculate best friend, who is always
aghast at the stains on your baggy jumper, will have
her own kid and look even worse.*

*That the person who invented jogging is eventually
forced to admit it makes you die younger.*

In Martin Scorsese's *The King of Comedy* (1983), fantasist Rupert
Pupkin imagines himself a superstar comedian appearing on *The
Jerry Langford Show*. They bring in a surprise guest: his old head-
master! The high school principal approaches the star timidly,
even reverentially. Pupkin makes a great show of not recognizing
him (remember: this is all going on in Pupkin's head), but the
principal persists. He wants to apologize personally, in front of the
whole country, on behalf of everyone who thought Pupkin
wouldn't amount to anything, and beg his forgiveness, and thank
him for the meaning he has given everyone's lives.

When it comes to those who have wronged us, most of us
secretly want to see—or at least, imagine—the precise moment

that person realizes they have transgressed: the confusion, the horror, the regret crumpling their faces. And in fact, because we know how important these moments are, we often provide them for others too. Most of us automatically signal to others that we realize we've made a mistake. We mutter remonstrations to ourselves when we trip, or make a show of cringing when our phone rings in the library, or pantomime holding our head in our hands in shame when we've made a mistake in the car.

These tiny specks of behavior are admissions of guilt, demonstrations that we are suffering already and do not need to be punished further. When people attempt to brazen out their failure, things get more complicated. When the contestant on a reality TV show gets a terrible score from the judges, and seems not to care, even implying that the judges don't know what they're talking about, then we respond with wincing and scoffing, the exquisite torture known in Spain as *vergüenza ajena* (or sympathetic shame). But if that contestant looks crestfallen, with a slight tremble on their lips? Then: *awwww, maybe they weren't so bad* may be our predictable response.

If we can't actually witness our erstwhile tormenters broken and shamed upon realizing the gravity of their mistake, then we must, of course, imagine it. In "Who's Laughing Now," Jessie J sings about the classmates who once teased and bullied her trying to befriend her now that she is rich and famous and living in LA. This is nothing. Sue Townsend's celebrated diarist Adrian Mole, aged 13¾, is one of the great masters of these fantasy comeuppances, obsessed with elaborate scenarios in which people who have diminished him are confronted with the error of their ways. The geography teacher will be sorry when Adrian grows up to be a Famous Intellectual. Pandora will cry herself to sleep when Adrian, tanned and knowledgeable, returns from traveling the world and she realizes she missed her chance to marry him. The school bully Barry Kent will end up in prison, where he will read Adrian's PhD thesis on the relative stupidity of larger youths compared to smaller youths and feel ashamed at his sniveling inferiority.

We imagine their pain and shame and think: *maybe they won't be so arrogant next time.* Though look more closely and our self-satisfaction will be curled at the edges in a little twinge of fear. Because we all know that nothing is more likely to lead to a comeuppance than smugly gloating over someone else's.

In A. A. Milne's Winnie the Pooh story "In which Tigger is Unbounced," it is a summer afternoon, and Rabbit, Pooh and Piglet sit outside Pooh's front door talking about the new arrival in their small community, the irrepressible, exuberant Tigger. "In fact," Rabbit says as Pooh wakes up from his daydream, "Tigger is getting so bouncy nowadays that it's time we taught him a lesson... There's too much of him, that's what it comes to." Rabbit hatches a plan. They will take Tigger deep into the forest, lose him, and then come back to rescue him the next morning:

> "Why?" said Pooh.
> "Because he'll be a Humble Tigger. Because he'll be a Sad Tigger, a Melancholy Tigger, a Small and Sorry Tigger, an Oh-Rabbit-I-am-glad-to-see-you

Tigger. That's why...If we can make Tigger feel
Small and Sad just for five minutes, we will have
done a good deed."

Well, you can guess how it ends. Rabbit gets lost, and becomes
Small and Sorry. And Tigger, who lacks fear, along with all social
grace, rescues him.

5

Love

Siblings, sex and gossip

When the shiny new guy at work is caught looking at senior-citizen porn.

When our new housemate made us feel inadequate with tales of his rock 'n' roll lifestyle, and then we heard him being violently sick after four pints.

When we were kids and my brother developed an enraging affectation of rolling a matchstick around his mouth, positioning it between his teeth and strumming it while thinking. Sometimes for emphasis, he even took it out of his mouth and pointed at me with it. And then he swallowed it accidentally and our mom had to take him to the doctor.

When I go to interview the writer and psychotherapist Philippa Perry, I arrive at her house to find her having lost 6,000 words of her new book due to a computer malfunction. Even though she generously does not cancel, I can see the worry zigzagging over her forehead. She makes tea. And then she looks at me carefully. "Well? Are you feeling pleased at my misfortune?" I laugh. "Definitely not!" And at the time, I was pretty sure that was true (if anything, it just made me antsy about my own computer malfunctioning, so not exactly the empathic ideal either).

But later this struck me. I had felt surprisingly relaxed, even confident during the interview. Philippa may be an expert at putting people at their ease, but was it also possible that something about her crisis had made me unusually self-possessed?

We sip tea and she says: "It's a very beautiful thing when we're on a team or in a family and we're all moving together like starlings in a sky...But humans aren't like a flock of starlings, and when we're pulling in two different directions, and when your direction wins at the expense of the other person's direction, it feels good."

"Why?" I ask.

"Love," she shrugs, like it's obvious.

"I was once on a walk near my country house with my dad and my daughter," she tells me. "It's a reasonably isolated cottage... My daughter was six or seven. She and her friends would take picnics and go out on adventures on their own. On this walk, I came across what I recognized to be one of *my* Sainsbury drink cartons and *my* napkins rotting among the dung... 'What's that, Flo?' I said, pointing to the wrappers. 'Sorry, I forgot to clear up,' says my daughter. So we cleared up.

"I was not feeling charged about it at all. And my father said to me, 'How honest of Flo to own up like that straight away.' And I still felt neutral. But then he said, 'Not like your nieces, they can be really sneaky.' That's my sister's children. And I felt such pleasure. A great waft, a powerful charge of pleasure which I had not felt when he was merely praising her for her honesty. But when he compared her to my rival's children, my sister's children...

"And then I thought, 'What's that about?,' and I did not feel so great about it. This is how we were brought up, always compared to each other like that. One good, one bad.

"It felt like ... *power* when my father compared me to my sister. It felt like 'I'm going to get the crown of the tribe.' It's ridiculous."

RIVALS

When your popular, sporty brother got a detention.

Or lost the expensive new headphones he'd been begging for all year.

Or at a family lunch, your parents mention how lovely your brother's children are, and it absolutely, definitely sounds like they're really saying that your brother's kids are nicer than your kids, and then your brother's kid comes in sobbing with chocolate smeared all over his face and screams: "Grandma's a fucking bitch!"

It is hard to point to the precise moment that competitiveness awakens. One moment you are enjoying a perfectly convivial conversation with a sibling; the next moment some piece of news has triggered a bristling feeling and an urge to outdo, or else left you with the roiling, lurching feeling that you are being left behind. No wonder that in these moments we are so happy to take any news of a failure as a win, and breathe a sigh of relief.

For Perry, the roots of competitiveness lie in our earliest family relationships and our deepest need for love. Survival is at stake. For our ancestors, a parent's approval might have meant the difference between surviving or not. Even in a comfortable, modern Western home, where there are enough resources to go around, we still have an in-built sense that love and approval are worth fighting for — even if that fight is cloaked in secrecy and shame.

Some of this distaste can be traced back to the last decades of the nineteenth century, when the concept of "sibling rivalry" first appeared. Where in the past, unhappy sibling relationships had been seen as a deviation rather than a norm, a new breed of medical professional, the child psychologist, argued that children were perpetually locked in a battle for resources and attention. But since rivalrous children were thought to grow into uncooperative, "difficult" adults with low "self-esteem" (another new concept at this time), middle-class parents were urged to be vigilant, and parcel out attentions and praise equally. And children, meanwhile, were taught to suppress their gloating. As the psychologist Felix Adler put it in his 1893 *Moral Instruction of Children*: "Do not triumph in your brother's disgrace, or taunt him with his failings" (or as was more familiar to me: "And you can wipe that smirk off your face too, young lady").

Of course, we grow up. Yet, even in the most apparently harmonious adult sibling relationships, there is the occasional furtive jostle, and a little squib of glee when our erstwhile rival falters, and we are left feeling, as Philippa put it, like king of the tribe, or at the very least, not quite as bad as before. Iris Murdoch must have recognized this feeling; in her novel *A Severed Head*, Martin Lynch-Gibbon imagines sharing the news that his wife has left him with his sister, also divorced. She would "maintain a conventional air of distress," he predicted, but this attitude would mask a "not yet diagnosed sense of all being exceptionally well with the world."

Such feelings, however, are not necessarily the result of having parents who have compared and contrasted us. They are amplified because we live in a world where it is inevitable that we measure ourselves against the next person, and where sometimes our only chance of seeing ourselves as successful is if the competition has lost.

OTHER PEOPLE MUST FAIL

Conventional wisdom teaches us to look within, to ignore what other people are doing, and plow our own furrows. And yet most of us at one time or another have found ourselves scrutinizing another's apparently successful life, and wondering whether our own measures up. Most grin with recognition at that homily, attributed to Ghengis Khan, Gore Vidal and others, that "it is not enough that I succeed—others must fail." It is hardly virtuous, but is it true that our own achievements feel so much more satisfying if we can compare them to someone else's failure? Philippa and I conduct an experiment.

Philippa writes a monthly agony aunt column in a British magazine, a job she really loves. As far as she is aware, there was no other candidate for this job. So we pretend I had pitched for the job, just to see how it feels:

Philippa:	I pitched that they should have an agony aunt at *Red* magazine.
Me:	Oh I pitched that they should have an agony aunt too.
Philippa:	What happened?
Me:	Well, I wrote to them, we went out for lunch. I did a sample. I didn't hear anything back. So I sent a couple of emails, and then it got embarrassing, so...I thought they'd probably dropped the idea.
Philippa:	No, they gave the column to me.
Me:	Oh.

"Oh, this is great!" shouts Philippa, clapping her hands and laughing. "I feel great! I *do* feel better than when I thought I'd just got it and no one else wanted it. Let's do it again!" This time, we pretend she had been pursuing my husband, Michael:

Philippa:	You know that Michael, God, I used to really like him.
Me:	Er—
Philippa:	He was so sexy. I dropped loads of hints, but—
Me:	Er, so—
Philippa:	I guess he just wasn't interested.
Me:	You know, Michael and I got together. Actually, we're married.

She's right, it is *great*. "Did you feel sorry for me *at all*?" asks Philippa. "No!" I hear myself shouting, giddy with excitement. And I too want to do it all over again.

"This is a terrible part of human nature," says Philippa. "And *we* are *very* good people. Not like those other people."

It comes down to this: How do we measure our own worth? There are many studies which suggest that we are happiest when we are surrounded by people who have slightly less than us. When psychologists asked in one study, "Would you prefer it if other people's children were less or more good-looking than your children?," most said they would be happier in a world where everyone else's children were less good-looking than their own. "Even if your child is ugly?" "Yes," they replied.

This doesn't entirely surprise me. Endless attempts to compare accomplishments or money or status may seem distasteful. Yet everyone who has written about human psychology, from Aristotle to Rousseau, Montaigne to de Beauvoir, has emphasized that living in small, interdependent groups inevitably also brings with it jockeying for power and competing over resources. Feeling a

stab of triumph when someone fails at something you are successful at is inevitable.

As I pack away my notebook and struggle into my hat and
gloves, Philippa admits that she is starting to feel a bit uncomfortable about all the Schadenfreude she has admitted to. "I feel a bit
dirty. I feel that way when you look back over your day and you
think: What will that person think of me now?" "I feel a bit over-
exposed," I agree. I remember all those other conversations I've
had with people about Schadenfreude, which have ended with a
similar admission of awkwardness. Or a promise not to divulge.
When we started swapping tales to think about this book, my editor even suggested we operate in conditions of strict confidential-
ity: the first rule of Schadenfreude Club...

No doubt there is the fear of revealing our true unpleasant
selves, the shameful possibility that we might not be "very good
people" after all. Perhaps there is a sense of transgression which
can be exciting but frightening. Certainly, the fear that we will be
exposed comes hand in hand with not wanting to offend people,
or rupture the bonds of trust that keep us safe and help us survive.
We are trapped, both by our shame and by our better judgment.
So what should we do?

"What we should do is notice it. Learn to recognize it," says
Perry. "Admit to it, even to other people. What we need to understand when we detect a glimmer of Schadenfreude is that 'What
I'm doing is making myself feel more secure at the expense of
someone else's insecurity, and I don't need to do it.' It's a natural
thing to do, but once we're aware of it we can arrest it. We don't

need to do it; no one does. It doesn't give us more love. It doesn't make us more attractive.'"

I agree with her, and resolve to do what she suggests, and learn to have those conversations (the Afterword, p. 41, has her suggestion for what they might sound like). She's right, I think. Schadenfreude is simply a cheap way of feeling better about yourself. Even if it hurts no one else, it might well leave you feeling a little sordid.

Her words ring in my ears: "It doesn't give us more love. It doesn't make us more attractive."

But then I get home and turn on my computer. And in my email inbox is an article that says Schadenfreude makes us more attractive. And gets us love.

HOW TO BE HAPPY AND BOOST YOUR SELF-ESTEEM

*When your ex-friend lands your dream job
in a record company and won't stop boasting
about it on Facebook — and then the
company goes bust.*

*When your self-satisfied colleague becomes
semi-famous because of his blog, and he is booked to
speak in a fancy bookshop — and then they cancel the
event because no one bought tickets.*

*When you have a bad date, and then you read this: A
woman met a man on Tinder, and when they went
back to his house, she went to the loo. But she found
to her dismay that her poo did not flush. So, she
panicked and tried to THROW IT OUT THE
WINDOW. But she hadn't realized that the window
had two layers of glass, so the poo got stuck in the gap
between them. And then she climbed in after it, and
got stuck too. And the fire service had to rescue her.*

The hypothesis was simple: seeing a sexual competitor fail enhances
our perception of our own sexual attractiveness. A group of students read stories about their peers suffering some misfortune—
being caught cheating on an exam or having a bad haircut, for
example. When female students read about another female student experiencing some misfortune related to her appearance
(gaining weight, a spot), they reported higher levels of Schadenfreude than when she suffered another setback, such as getting a
bad mark on an essay. When male students read about another
male student experiencing a loss in what the psychologists called
"status" (missing an exam; giving a foolish answer in a seminar),
they reported more pleasure than when he had, say, gained weight.
The study's authors concluded that, among university students at
least, the strongest Schadenfreude is felt when a direct sexual

competitor meets some misfortune linked to qualities *convention-ally associated with their gender's attractiveness.*

These pretty dispiriting findings led the psychologists to a more intriguing possibility. Might Schadenfreude have evolved as an adaptive behavior, helping us in our quest to find a mate? It's not just that getting a few spotty cheats out of the way will help us secure the prize. It's also that Schadenfreude gives a little boost. A potential rival's mishap makes us think we are sexier by compari-son. And when we rate our attractiveness more highly, we inevita-bly feel more confident and willing to approach the whole awful business of flirting and asking people on dates with gusto and vim. And who wouldn't want to have sex with someone like that?

The idea that we gain some psychological benefit from other people's disadvantages is not new. During the Second World War a sociologist named Samuel A. Stouffer, who was studying army morale, noticed that African American soldiers stationed in the southern U.S. described themselves as happier and more satisfied than those stationed in the North, despite the fact that the South in the 1940s remained racially segregated. Since there was little objective difference in their conditions, Stouffer realized that the soldiers were basing their appraisal of their quality of life on a comparison. Black soldiers stationed in the South compared their situation with local African Americans, for whom life was very hard—and felt comparatively lucky. Black soldiers stationed in the North felt comparatively worse off than the rest of the local black population, who enjoyed more liberty than them. Stouffer called his insight the "relative deprivation theory," concluding that it may in fact be more painful to be relatively deprived than to be actually deprived (or, as Marx put it, "A house may be large or small. As long as the surrounding houses are equally small, it satisfies all social demands for a dwelling. But let a palace arise beside the little house, and it shrinks from a little house to a hut.").

In the 1980s the psychologist Tom Wills took the idea of relative deprivation and gave it a new twist. He hypothesized that people can—and often do—bump up their self-esteem by comparing themselves to people *less* fortunate than themselves. Wills noticed there were a variety of strategies. One is privately derogating a person to cheer yourself up: *they might be paid more than me, but my job is far more meaningful.* Another is deliberately undermining their achievements to their face: *Congratulations on your pay rise!* And then later: *Do you know how many people your company made redundant last year?* The most common technique is to seize any opportunity you get to hear details about someone who is going through a worse time than you: *Oh, he got fired from his job? That's terrible... What happened?* There have always been people who gravitate toward those having a hard time, or like to gossip about the latest developments in a neighbor's tragedy. Now it had a name—"downward social comparison": enhancing your self-regard by comparing yourself to those worse off than you.

With its flawless, filtered images, and endless anecdotes about exciting parties, social media is generally blamed for making us feel worse about ourselves. Far less is spoken about the opportunities it offers to ramp up our self-estimation by comparing ourselves to those worse off—and sometimes at the most vulnerable moments in our lives.

A year after Wills published his theory, another social psychologist, Shelley E. Taylor, and her team published the results of a long-term study with cancer patients. Taylor noticed that during their interviews, patients, unprompted, would often compare themselves to imaginary others who were worse off. *Imagine not having a family to help you.* Or: *Imagine having to travel for miles to get to the hospital.* Such imaginary comparisons require significant effort and invention, and suggested to Taylor that they are part of the psychic toolkit that we use to help us cope with threats of the most terrifying kind. They create gratitude: *It could be worse*... (or, as we were told growing up, *Think of the starving children in Africa*). It recalls Lucretius' theory, discussed in Chapter 2, that "It's sweet to know from what misfortunes you are free." The difference is, the patients Taylor was interviewing were inventing the people who were worse off than them.

More recent research looking at people's use of health message boards suggests a more complex picture. People in worse situations than you can give some measure of consolation, but hearing about more serious diagnoses can also prompt anxiety. The control we feel over our lives seems to be a factor. Wills thought that people with lower self-esteem were most likely to gravitate to stories of other people's suffering because they had greater need for the psychic boost. But recent studies suggest that it may be confident people who have the most to gain from other people's problems, since they usually also think they have more control over their lives, and so see their comparative good fortune as deserved in some way. Conversely, the less confident, who feel a lack of control, see someone worse off and may think they will eventually share the same fate (especially if the unfortunate person is someone they strongly identify with).

Clearly, we are capable of engaging with other people's bad news in many different and complex ways. But the fact that we sometimes benefit from hearing about other people's crises is not a secret. In fact, from time to time we even comply, willingly offering up our own miseries in an attempt to help strangers feel better about theirs.

MY HORRIBLE LIFE

Tagging myself in a picture of my ex-boyfriend's wedding while trying to zoom in on the bride's face.

Falling asleep on a bus journey, and on waking up, a kid saying, "Daddy! The drooling lady is awake!"

Drunkenly chatting up someone in a pub, who finally coughs and politely points out that I have toilet paper trailing out of the back of my trousers.

There is a notion that when people are down they need jollying along or distraction. This is deeply misguided. The best medicine is hearing about something so laughably awful that your own problems look daft by comparison.

In 2008, in France, three coders set up a site called *viedemerde. fr* ("shit life"), but translated into English as "fuck my life" (fmylife.com), which enacted this same phenomenon on a global scale. It invited visitors to post anecdotes of their life fails, the more disastrous the better. Tales poured in, from the minor (people retweeting themselves) to the major (discovering that the old lady snoozing on their shoulder on the bus had, in fact, died). Readers vote whether the writer "deserved" their bad luck, or, if truly, their life "sucks."

The site captured an ironic, disaffected mood at the onset of a global economic recession and ongoing war in Iraq. In the face of global catastrophes, it offered displays of adolescent melodrama and indignation combined with epic levels of competitive whining about relatively minor bits of hard luck. FML has been criticized for helping to create a culture of baffled passivity and victimhood, sapping energy in already disaffected times by inviting people to self-identify as "losers." This seems ungenerous. I can't help admiring the way that, instead of trying to make people envy them, the FML contributors offer readers the chance to feel some consoling Schadenfreude at their expense, the disasters they post about almost certainly leaving readers feeling a little bit happier about how their own days are going.

We often do this, inviting others to laugh at our failures. Think about when we join a new sports team, or start a new job — most of us fall back on self-deprecatory jokes in order to ease our transition, and in the hope that they'll help us be seen as less of a threat. Gallows humor also relies on this ability to put one's own suffering front and center, and make it laughable — a way of coping for both yourself and your audience. In the late 2000s, a choir was set up in Durban, South Africa, to support patients living with HIV/AIDS. With the disease deeply taboo, the only jokes circulating about it were demeaning. The choir members repurposed these jokes, scoffing at each other's symptoms, showboating about whose were more serious, and teasing the worst off. Inviting people to laugh at our pain can be a way of managing it—perhaps even, as that study on belly laughter and slapstick discussed in Chapter 1 found, raising our tolerance.

More than this, mocking pain remains central to many traditional medical practices across the globe. While she was living among the Makushi of North Rupununi in Guyana, the anthropologist Laura Scherberger injured her knee playing football with the women of the village, and one suggested she go to see Magnus, the local *piyaman* (or shaman). After a painful walk through the savannah, she found Magnus and his wife, "Granny," in a small dark house crowded with their relatives and surrounded by dense rain forest. Magnus explained that Laura's pain was now happily "married" to her knee, and must be persuaded to leave. As Magnus performed his ritual, Granny rose from her hammock and threw insults at the pain, cursing and ridiculing it—and others, including children, joined in, giggling wildly (partly at the pain, and partly it seems because Granny's clothes had inexplicably fallen off). At the end of the ceremony, when asked if her knee felt better, the anthropologist, somewhat surprised, discovered that it did.

Most of us won't experience a *piyaman* ceremony, but all of us will recognize that, when we feel miserable, a little teasing, sensitively done by a trusted friend, can help. And most of us willingly offer up our worst disasters so that our friends, in their moments of need, can feel less desperate. These moments speak of solace and camaraderie, a shared understanding of life's suffering and the desire to even temporarily alleviate it. They remind us that what appears flawless rarely is, and other people's apparent advantages do not indemnify them against the indignities of a badly timed fart or no one showing up to their birthday party. And this is important, to know that other people experience their vulnerabilities and moments of despair. Because it's not just us who fail. Everyone does.

6

Envy

Friends, celebrities and Z-listers

When a friend spends a fiver on a bottle of "raw water" and then promptly spills it down her front.

Or decides parking restrictions are for wimps, and gets clamped.

When she is walking and texting far too dynamically, and collides with a tree.

Or gets a new phone and won't stop showing off about all its whizzy features, and then there is a story in the news about those phones spontaneously exploding.

When she posts a picture all over social media of her and her new boyfriend cutely lying on an autumnal forest floor, and there is a piece of poo just inches away from their heads.

He leans in across the dinner table, the candles flickering against the empty bottles of wine. "The thing that I get, and I mean *a lot*, is when my friends do better than me. I hate it."

I laugh, and then laugh again more awkwardly. We are at dinner at the house of a school friend of my husband's, who has become a very successful lawyer: his life is very different from ours. Another of my husband's friends is there, and he is drunk enough to keep going. He gestures around the dining table. "I love my friends. I really do. But then, their kids do better at school. Or they earn more money. They live in..." He sweeps his eyes over the polished concrete floor and epic windows. "They drive nice cars. Somehow they have time to do exercise. They're not going bald. We used to be on an equal footing. Sometimes I was even better than them. Got better marks on my essays. Was the first one in our group to get a girlfriend. And there you are remembering their birthdays and organizing their stag parties and suddenly they've sprinted right past you." He wipes his hand across his hair. I try not to look too closely at how much it's thinning. "I hate that they're so successful. And I feel so guilty about it, so guilty." The table unfortunately goes silent at this point. "What? She's writing a book on Schadenfreude," he mock-pleads, though I can see the pink rising at his throat. "I would never, *ever*, feel happy if things went badly for any of *you*."

We feel Schadenfreude at painful surprises, or when we think we might win. We feel it when we see someone who deserves their comeuppance, and when smug people suffer. We feel it toward our siblings, and sometimes even strangers let us feel it on their behalf.

But few things elicit such guilty spasms of delicious Schaden-freude as the disappointments of our most successful friends.

Montaigne wrote that true friendship was rare and pure. For Ralph Waldo Emerson, it required a true sympatico, "an absolute running of two souls into one." Our friends are supposed to share our triumphs and commiserate with our sorrows, but everyone knows it doesn't always go exactly like that. Perhaps you feel pride at being able to console; detect a little undertow of smugness that *your* shoulder was the one picked to cry on; enjoy the chance to reimagine yourself as Helpful, Kind and Good in a Crisis. *We* know that self-congratulatory pleasure can coexist with compassion, but not everyone does. The eighteenth-century philosopher Adam Smith was so indignant about the idea that any of his so-called friends might not be entirely sympathetic, he vowed that "If you have either no fellow-feeling for the misfortunes I have met with, or none that bears any proportion to the grief which distracts me . . . we can no longer converse." One can't help thinking that, had Smith known the truth, he might have been rather lonely.

It's hard to imagine anyone gloating when a close friend meets catastrophe—a bereavement, a messy divorce, a child's illness. But at some point or another, most of us have experienced a tiny, guilty spasm of delight when something a friend has been showing off about has gone wrong. Their glamorous, freshly tiled bathroom leaves you feeling instantly inadequate. Until, that is, you notice their husband's special deodorant to counteract excessive sweating. Or they insist on demonstrating how their new blender, with the

3.0-horsepower motor and five variable-speed settings, BPA-free touchpad interface and illuminated LCD screen, makes the perfect fish stock. And forget to put the lid on properly. When their new car makes spooky groans, or their cashmere jumper is being snacked on by moths. When they're super-cool and take their kids off to a music festival ("No big deal!" "It'll be fun!"), and then come back ashen-faced and looking as if they've been fighting at the Somme. Or their cat, toward whom they lavish attention befitting a despot leader of a small country, rejects their lap for yours. All of these relatively inconsequential misfortunes are salvations for you.

Of course, *of course*, you want the bathroom and the blender, the car, the cashmere and the cat. Yes, *you too* want to be the sort of person who goes to music festivals with your kids. We envy in others what we desire for ourselves, and the life we imagine is, by rights, ours ("envy pits potter against potter" wrote Aristotle). The intense glee of Schadenfreude is a momentary compensation for everything they have that we lack. And it leaves us that bit more sprightly as a result.

François de La Rochefoucauld, a seventeenth-century French nobleman whose acerbic and witty maxims have earned him a reputation as the destroyer of vain delusions, knew this to be true. It is not hard to cope with our friends' disappointments, he wrote. It is their triumphs which are difficult to bear. And so, "in the adversity of our best friends we always find something that does not displease us."

When I came to check this La Rochefoucauld reference, I noticed that he had ended up withdrawing this home truth from later editions of his *Maxims*, published during his lifetime. For all his famous candor, he had clearly got the willies that his friends might read it and hate him. Wimp!

And then I paused. And hurriedly fired off an email to Richard H. Smith, a psychologist at the University of Kentucky whose articles on politics and Schadenfreude I had been reading (discussed in the final chapter): "When I tell my friends what I'm writing about, they laugh at first, and then start looking uncomfortable when I explain what it all means," I confessed.

"Oh yes," he replied, "the same happened to me."

STARE AND COMPARE

When a friend insists that cooking rice is easy—and then ends up with a glutinous, burnt mess.

When your show-off flatmate has been going on about a forthcoming TV appearance for ages—and then gets bumped for a YouTube-star shih tzu.

When a Facebook friend declares himself to be in an open relationship with his girlfriend and smugly implies he never gets jealous because he is so liberated and emotionally mature—and then a week later you find out they split up when he was caught going through her phone.

Perhaps the hardest moment in any friendship is when lifestyles diverge. When the person you waitressed with through college, counting out your pennies for a packet of cigarettes, is now earning a six-figure salary and living in Hampstead. Or while you are still a wage-slave in the first company that hired you, still single and still waking up hungover on a Sunday morning, your best friend has adopted three children, moved to the country, runs marathons and earns his money "life coaching via Skype."

These successes inevitably bring mixed feelings. The worry that you're being left behind or not being ambitious enough. The resentment that it all seems to have come to them so effortlessly. The fear that you no longer fit in their glossy new life, which leaves you oversensitive to every text message that goes unreplied, and each drink canceled at the last minute. Inadequacy, shot through with the suspicion of some unfairness that has led them to a gilded life while you scrabble around in the dirt, is the light into which delicate seedlings of Schadenfreude strain.

No wonder we seek to redress the balance, noticing, perhaps, their little failures in an effort to salve our fragile and threatened self-image. Like the fox in Aesop's fable who, finding himself unable to reach some delicious-looking grapes, declares them sour and inedible, we might tell ourselves that our friend's success has come at a horrible price, and that perhaps it is not a success after all — and fixate on their newfound misery. Perhaps your friend has had a massive promotion. You might mull it over and conclude: "But God, he looks so tired, it must be taking its toll." Or else we play that game. *You* know. That one after a night out with a friend whose life is infinitely better than yours? On the train home, you'll start enumerating the reasons why their life is actually a bit crap. "That house is *too* big, it's just impersonal." Or "I know he earns a lot, but those hours! And commuting every day to the city? I couldn't do it." Or "If I had their money, I wouldn't spend it on *that* (car/suit/TV)."

There is not as much shame as you'd think in such defenses, in wanting to smudge the friend's shine a little. In this age of perfectly curated and filtered lives on social media, seeing someone fail may be the only way to see them as human. Envy (from the Latin *invidia*, which means "looking upon") is the lust for other people's things, qualities or accomplishments (jealousy is a longing for people). And it feeds off glistening surfaces which obscure the mixed realities underneath. Envy amplifies other people's successes, and makes our own seem paler by comparison — as Cassius discovers with devastating effects in *Julius Caesar*. He burnishes Caesar, once his childhood friend and equal and now the most powerful man in Rome, with a godlike power, and casts himself as pathetic by comparison: "He doth bestride the narrow world / Like a colossus, and we petty men / Walk under his huge legs and peep about / To find ourselves dishonorable graves."

We've all been there. When you stupidly look at a friend's "My Adventures" album, with selfie after selfie by the pool sipping cocktails, climbing snowy mountains, doing yoga in a monastery, and feel wretched that your own Christmas involved sitting on Auntie Maureen's couch eating toast, again. A flicker of Schadenfreude can neutralize the envy, catching it before it turns into hostility and spite. And there's one area where we need its compensations most of all: in our conflicted, profoundly masochistic relationship to celebrities.

CELEBRITY FAILS

When a boyishly charming actor is caught receiving a blow job from a prostitute on Sunset Boulevard.

When a Hollywood hunk boasts about doing all his own stunts. "But it says here you can't swim!" replies the chat show host.

When a supermodel in towering heels trips on the runway.

When I read a celebrity interview, there is always some fleeting moment when I vaguely think that the A-list Hollywood actress could be my friend. Celebrity journalists are good at that. There's usually some "candid" detail: willowy model loathes exercise and licks the fondant from Oreos; famous actress's school run is "chaos." These moments lull me into a sense that we are equals. But then, in the next sentence, I read that they are buying a house in the Bahamas and wearing Valentino to the Oscars, and the space between us, which had momentarily contracted, expands so suddenly and violently that it is dizzy-making.

People have always been fascinated by the lives of the rich and famous, especially when they attempt to slither around the rules.

The hugely popular "broadside ballads," sung on street corners and in pubs between the sixteenth and nineteenth centuries, titillated with stories of murder and comeuppance, and loved a sudden twist of the wheel of fortune. One of the most popular, "The Fower Maries" (or "Four Marys"), told of an aristocratic beauty, a lady's maid to Mary Queen of Scots, who had an affair with the king, got pregnant, murdered the newborn infant and then set off to a party — whereupon she was promptly marched off to the scaffold and hung for her crime. The story was probably apocryphal, but real life also offered plenty of tidbits if you knew where to look. In 1751, the wife of Italian dilettante actor and writer Marquis Francesco Albergati Capacelli attempted to get her marriage annulled by declaring her husband impotent. We can still read the divorce-court proceedings that caused so much salacious glee at the time. Capacelli, brimming with indignation, called on his manservant as witness, who testified that "on three or four occasions I saw the said marquis getting out of bed with a perfect erection of the male organ."

The craving to see the mighty fall — and feel some superiority as a result — may be age-old, but modern celebrity has its own bitter logic. Scorned and taunted in *Us Weekly*, *Popbitch* and *MailOnline*, their marriage breakdowns, addictions and DUIs a source of frenzied speculation, our attitude to celebrities encapsulates the worst excesses of our Age of Schadenfreude. *Celebrity mildly disappointed after ordering wrong soup.* Meh. *Celebrity crashes car after discovering she is being betrayed by best friend who slept with her boyfriend shortly after cancer scare.* That's the ticket. What drives this savage desire to see them in the grip of such spectacular crises?

Where a friend's disappointment might help us manage their comparative success, digging into a celebrity's pain does more than anesthetize our own relative lack of beauty and talent. It has the quality of a punishment too. Unlike the aristocrats of the past, modern celebrities are rarely born into the immense privilege and influence they enjoy. We sense, somewhere, among it all, that they might have once been much like us (or, had our stars aligned very differently, we might have been them). On the one hand, we love a rags-to-riches tale, or the idea that underneath it all "they're just ordinary lads from Manchester," and crave a feeling of closeness to them. On the other, we hate them for how much we idolize and admire them, and wait eagerly in the wings for those moments when their entitlement to the high status they enjoy is tested — and they fail, the more spectacularly the better.

Perhaps they are filmed drunkenly spewing a vile racist rant at the side of the road. Or are suspected of trying to steal their costar's husband. Sometimes we suspect them of greedily trying to get more attention — for instance, by daring to have political opinions — and we eagerly wait to pounce on each misspelled tweet, or their confusion about the situation in Iberia or Liberia (or possibly, Ibiza), they can't remember which. We love to read about the shabby details that push through the glitz, not so much because we want to see these celebrities as human, but because we want to see them disqualified.

Part of this is the pleasure at seeing them self-destruct, tall poppies picking their own petals off, and laying waste to those talents that got them there in the first place. Genuine Britney Spears fans are traumatized by pictures of her stumbling out of McDonald's, her head shaved, mascara pooling on her blotchy cheeks. But for the rest of us? We might notice an obscene glint of exultant pleasure, as if her mental breakdown were evidence that in her meteoric rise to global pop domination Britney had shot too close to the sun.

We reserve our most exultant Schadenfreude for the "famous for being famous." I remember when the first series of *Big Brother* came out. Those were relatively innocent times: the program felt like some kind of twisted psychology experiment. And then there was Nasty Nick. He lied, he manipulated, he boasted. He said he had spent three years in the territorial army, so the producers rigged up a military-style assault course in the garden as a group task; all the housemates managed the monkey bars fine except Nick, who lurched and wriggled across and eventually slipped.

Nasty Nick taught the TV companies that what people actually enjoy watching is other people trying to get away with lies and manipulation, and being caught. They figured out that what pushed the ratings through the roof was fame-hungry weirdos, and learned to capitalize on the Schadenfreude they created. Of course, it wasn't just the TV execs who learned to love the Schadenfreude. Contestants also started playing the game, hoping to become the focus of media attention through their failure. Think of Paul Burrell, Lady Diana's former butler, who on *I'm a Celebrity... Get Me Out of Here* camped up his squeamishness hoping to create drama—and just looked foolish as a result. As with fail videos, any whiff of a setup breeds disdain: we want our oddballs genuinely unaware of how badly they are coming across.

There are few arenas of life in which Schadenfreude is exploited so nakedly for financial gain as celebrity rags, with their constant demand for rise-and-fall stories, of overnight fame and fortune, of hubris and humiliation. We know they manipulate and intrude and, often, terrify the celebrities they stalk, and yet we are willing to turn the volume down on our scruples for an amusing tale of a celebrity's botched plastic surgery. You're a creature of "contempt and malice…you're a slimy scandal…you are a national disgrace!," rages New York columnist Hunsecker to sleazy celebrity PR man Falco in the 1957 film *Sweet Smell of Success*. He might well have been talking to us.

But here's the thing. We might scoff at a celebrity's downfall, and believe, perhaps, that our scorn lessens their power. We might even think, "Ah, that's him finished," with the vague notion that we have sacked him, since celebrities rely on that most mercurial thing, "public approval," for their pay check, and we, after all, are the public. But this, of course, is wishful thinking. Celebrities and their PRs ultimately know how to ride the waves of Schadenfreude, provoking, absorbing and reappropriating it as required. The baby-faced TV presenter who drinks too much, or the actor exposed for diva-like behavior on set does not withdraw humiliated and shamed, never to be seen again (and we might not feel great if they did). Eventually, they'll be back on the sofa, clutching a tissue, with tales of treatment, and admissions of guilt, and apologies glistening on their lips. We might think our Schaden-freude is our power. Truth is, they've stolen it right back from us, our little piece of superiority returned with a kiss. And so the question that we might find ourselves wondering about, if we care to notice it, is this: Does gloating over someone else's failures *ever change anything at all*?

7

Mutiny

Employees, bosses and rebels

*When Declan, the office Buddhist,
loses it at the photocopier.*

*When Tim from accounts can't remember
how to do long division.*

*When Samira won't stop aggressively typing even
when you're talking to her, so you look over her
shoulder, and all she's writing is: ad;flkjals;dkjf
easllwejjo iasfdk kneessasllee.*

*When Ben's phone rings, and he is bunking
off (again), and he asks you to cover by answering
his phone and pretending to be him, so you do,
and it is the results of his STD test.*

When Lucy's "emotional support hamster" bit her.

We drifted one by one into the meeting room on the fourth floor. The light was fading, and no one had yet switched on the overheads. The caterers had already arrived with the "informal lunch" on platters, sad-looking sandwiches and some sliced fruit. My friend Mark peeled off the cellophane, and started to help himself, and then we all joined in, a little giddy with the prospect of free food.

The view from the window took in most of the east of the city, and it was possible to see the newest tallest building going up, red lights festooning the cranes, purplish clouds drifting across. An airplane. There was small talk: *Good Christmas?* The heating was too high. We were waiting.

The vice-chancellor of our university was coming to "meet" us. "Informally." For a whole half an hour, which, we had been told by our head of department (over email, but the smirk was definitely detectable), was an unprecedentedly long audience to be granted. Had anyone actually ever met our new boss? Screwed-up faces. Shrugs. The older ones stared at their iCals like it was all a monumental waste of their time. Some of the younger ones were keener, hair brushed, smart trousers, as if in that meeting an impression might be made and a glittering future in senior management secured. The rest, me included, were just suspicious for no other reason than that this was the person in charge and it was our moral duty to mistrust them.

The catering man returned, this time with a thermos of coffee and the posh biscuits. And at that same moment, the VC arrived, ushered in by our manager, who looked harried and servile. Mark turned toward me, raised one of his enormous spidery eyebrows and jogged his head. I looked, took a moment to register, and grinned. Our VC was trailing a bit of toilet paper from her shoe.

THE IDEAL WORKER

Some coworkers are our conspirators and allies: they know all the most important details of our lives—when our dentist appointment is, why we can't buy a pair of shoes that fits, the punch lines of our best jokes. Others are our gossip buddies and box-set experts. Then there are the ones we say "hi" to in the lift. Some irritate, with the way they pick their ears or pile up mugs on their desk, or get inexplicably defensive every time you mention the strange smell coming out of the recycling bin near their desk.

But there is always one—at least one—who is our nemesis. The one who beat us to the promotion we wanted, whose easy wit makes the boss laugh, the one whose career we watch from the corner of our eye, comparing our own against it. Their successes leave us with an oily nervousness in the stomach, a sense that we must either fold or fight (and are we even up to the latter?). No wonder that, when these people meet some work-based catastrophe—misremembering the boss's kid's name, or being overheard joking about Lucy in HR's mustache—we experience a secret clutch of satisfaction. Their stock has fallen. Ours might rise.

If you look at adverts on TV, you might believe that today's workplaces are thriving ecosystems of trust and mutual respect. Employees (usually portrayed as knowledge workers—software engineers, designers, architects or, improbably, academics) are open and enthusiastic, happy and productive. They take things on, and get things done, all while having an open and agreeable relationship with their colleagues and bosses, who in turn value their individual contributions. Gone are the divide-and-rule tactics of sadistic managers, the humiliating hazing rituals, the never-ending subterranean games of one-upmanship. The modern workplace aspires to teams not tyrannies, civility not scorn, bean-bags not bullies. In it, mistakes are simply "learning moments": admit it; move on.

Truth told, in an office, Schadenfreude can sprout and multiply prolifically. Sometimes we are explicitly encouraged to feed it. You know those horrible clip-art pictures of corporate people in suits high-fiving that are supposed to inspire? Behind each celebratory smile is another company's lost contract. Exhortations to "beat our competitors"? What else but an invitation to cheer when their profits plunge. Academics generally loathe the league tables of universities, which have become so much a feature of higher education in the UK today. But we still exchange little grins in the corridor at the news that our close competitor has slipped down the rankings—whether or not we've crawled up. When it comes to our team against another's, their mistakes are a little chink of light through which we might scramble, a triumph not so much for us as individuals, but for our tribe (about which, more in the next chapter).

Most workplace Schadenfreude is, of course, far more covert, and arises from the suspicion that we might be nudged out of the way, or some attempt at one-upmanship is being launched. When a colleague's radical new suggestion for holding meetings standing up is firmly knocked back, we inwardly smirk, happy to see her slapped down trying to outdo us. Or take that wholesome colleague who loudly encourages you to go outside for lunch, making you look bad (you don't want to; you want to stay hunched over your computer looking at shoes). He gets caught in a freak downpour, and has to wear his PE kit to the board meeting—and you, with an enthusiasm not hitherto witnessed, arrive promptly at the meeting with an expectant look on your face, ready to hear him explain his "unconventional appearance" to the Chair.

Some workplaces deliberately set colleagues against each other, using winner-takes-all competitions for bonuses, or displaying everyone's monthly targets in the hope that this will stir their employees into working harder and faster. In this environment, laughing at a colleague for missing their target can be friendly banter, a way of letting off steam, and acknowledging that the wheel of fortune keeps turning, and what's mine today might be yours tomorrow. But even if in less overtly competitive environments there's always *that* colleague, who was once on your level (you might even have had a slight edge) but who somehow (*how?*) knew to schmooze and flirt with the right people, to go to the right coffee shop and drink the same obscure coffee blend as your boss, who was always in the lift at the right moment, cracking the right kind of joke, who somehow managed to contrive to wear exactly the same brand of shoes as your boss had Literally Just Bought (you suspect foul play; secret camera in boss's bedroom?). Eventually, he is given a prestigious account, and becomes unbearable: new bike, restaurant lunches, *jogging*. So when, some months later, we discover that he has made a monumental mess of it, we crane to overhear snatches of the angry conversation with the boss—door closed, blinds down. We see him slope away in disgrace. We cheerfully notice that he has become a quieter, more somber version of himself. This happy ending—part justice, part revenge—is our triumph and vindication, allowing us to congratulate ourselves on our own, slower (it's true) but steady, ascent.

For many of us, however, work is a far more awkward blend of competitiveness and collegiality, our colleagues at once friends and threats. One moment we are exhorted to collaborate and share, the next we find ourselves being appraised and compared. It's confusing, leaving us unsure whether to support and help our colleagues on their path to success, or stand back and secretly hope it doesn't all work out *too* well since, when their stock falls, ours might rise. In our relationships with work colleagues, there is a faint echo of those sly childhood battles, fought covertly behind our parents' backs, where we must appear to be behaving harmoniously with our siblings while actually engaging in the kind of masterly one-upmanship that would make Machiavelli blush.

We might experience a faint spasm of a reprieve when a colleague fails to win that prize, or feel vindicated when their End of Year Review was rather less glowing than everyone expected. We mask it as scrupulously as we can, but we notice it all right, and, perhaps later, feel a little shoddy and uncomfortable and wonder that it was there at all. Luckily, however, things are much more straightforward when it comes to celebrating the embarrassing gaffes of our bosses.

BAD BOSS MEETS STICKY END

*When the boss tells everyone to smarten
up their appearance—not realizing her
jumper is on inside out.*

*When, on a company away-day to the seaside, the MD
goes for a swim in the icy sea, implies that the rest of us
are wimps for not joining in, and gets a cramp.*

*When a new chief executive ostentatiously removes his
office door with a speech about "Communication,
Communication, Communication." And then Health
and Safety makes him put the door back.*

We laugh at their jokes and compliment their new hairdos, stand up straight and do our best listening faces when they tell us something important. We phrase our objections as "suggestions" and plaster a smile over our fury when it turns out that we've been scheduled for the Saturday-night shift yet again. Yes, we are the pathetic masses, the employees, and we love seeing our bosses trip up from time to time.

Robert I. Sutton is an organizational psychologist and Stanford professor, as well as the bestselling author of *The No Asshole Rule* and *The Asshole Survival Guide*. Bob is ebullient and generous and a great deal of fun. He is also probably one of the world's most confided-in people on the subject of terrible bosses (or "assholes," Bob's preferred term). Every day, Bob will open his inbox and find three or four emails have arrived from complete strangers describing vain managers and vindictive supervisors, and CEOs who have let the deference and flattery go to their heads, and believe the rules no longer apply to them. Some are asshole bosses, throwing temper tantrums or chairs, abusing, threatening and demeaning. Others are more insidious, subtly putting us down with a slight sneer here, a moment of studied disinterest there. Bob's favorite emails, however, are tales of comeuppance.

"One of the places Schadenfreude really comes through," he chuckles, "is when you hear a story about how an asshole is brought down." There was the high-profile airline company who sacked an asshole in IT: "She talked about how great they all felt after he left. And then he got a job in a rival company, which was viewed as a horrible place to work," and that was even better. There was the radio producer whose boss kept stealing the food off her desk, so she eventually made some chocolates with a laxative and informed him after he'd eaten a handful. There was the CEO who was dismissed for racist bullying, her behavior then being splashed over the *New York Times*, disgracing her. Or the corporate lawyer's secretary who accidentally spilled some ketchup on her boss's trousers; he then hounded her to repay a £4 cleaning bill, even emailing to remind her while she was dealing with her mother's death and funeral. Eventually, she shared his emails online, and he, humiliated, resigned. "The arc of a really good story of bringing down the asshole is you not only get rid of them, but they suffer in other ways too."

Bob's books, though generous about what a good workplace might look like, swill in this vast reservoir of Schadenfreude. Again and again, Bob enjoys reminding us how people with bad bosses tune out, using "creative avoidance" or sick days, or else resign, creating expensive staff turnover. And the lesson is deeply satisfying: asshole bosses harm their businesses, their legacy and their own careers.

Reading these tales appealed to my sense of justice or karma (even the ones that sound a bit like urban legends, like the laxative sweets on the desk). But more than that, they gave me a sense of camaraderie, the same sort of plucky feeling I get from reading tales of tricksters outwitting their oppressors. From the spider Anansi to the mischevious Huehuecóyotl of Aztec myths, to Jack of "Jack and the Beanstalk," tricksters appear in many traditions. The resourceful Br'er Rabbit, for instance, cannily outwits the fox who has trapped him. "Please, Br'er Fox, don't fling me in the brier-patch," pleads the rabbit. Of course, the fox, eager to make the rabbit suffer, does precisely that—and the rabbit, quite at home amid thorns and brambles, makes his escape. Like trickster stories, "Bringing Down the Asshole" tales rouse us, make us feel nimble and bold. And this confidence is both the gift of Schadenfreude, and potentially its risk.

RESSENTIMENT

When your former boss, a bully who made your life miserable, applies for a job at your new company— and you get to email her to tell her she has not been selected for an interview.

When the janitor in your apartment block who reported you for smoking on the roof accidentally starts a fire in the basement with his cigarette end.

When your old teacher, who cruelly humiliated you in front of the whole class for not understanding fractions, is discovered to have faked his degree.

Among the darkest, most pessimistic works of Western philosophy is *On the Genealogy of Morality* written by the German philosopher Friedrich Nietzsche. It makes disturbing reading today, not least because of Nietzsche's unvarnished contempt—for women, the Jewish faith, black people and homosexuals in particular (Nietzsche, you may be unsurprised to read, was Hitler's favorite philosopher). Yet if one idea from the *Genealogy* has lingered, it is the phenomenon Nietzsche called *ressentiment*, from the French word for "resentment" or "rancor," and the role Schadenfreude plays in it.

When we are hurt or demeaned, our natural response is to fight back, says Nietzsche. But he believed that when people either by their nature or circumstances were unable to defend themselves—perhaps because of physical weakness, or fear of an immediate reprisal, or because they depend on the aggressor, as, for instance, with a boss or parent—the anger is repressed into a buried hostility. We sit and wait, perhaps believing ourselves to be virtuously forgiving and patient or loyal, but in fact becoming ever more embittered and venomous, nursing fruitless fantasies of retribution and poised to gain little moments of satisfaction where we can. "His soul *squints*," writes Nietzsche of the person consumed with *ressentiment,* "his mind loves dark corners, secret paths and back-doors." Schadenfreude is one such underhand strategy, a "revenge of the impotent," delivering the sensation of retaliation with none of the risk.

In Nietzsche's writing, Schadenfreude becomes connected to the weak and gutless, a cramped, meager feeling, inert and powerless. According to Nietzsche, it was women and other underdogs (Jews, black people, homosexuals) who were most prone, since they needed its empty consolations, and its ersatz feeling of power. This is the Schadenfreude of Bertie Wooster, whose benefactor, Aunt Agatha, is a constant menace in his life. She peers down her beaky nose, and chastises him for his feckless ways; he simpers, lies and agrees. So when Agatha accuses a hotel maid of stealing her pearls, and then the pearls are discovered in her bedroom drawer after all, well: "I don't know when I've had a more juicy moment," crows Bertie. "It was one of those occasions about which I shall prattle to my grandchildren...Aunt Agatha simply deflated before my eyes."

Wooster's satisfaction may feel good but it is ultimately unproductive. Nothing changes in his relationship with Agatha: he goes back to praying she won't visit, and she goes back to lording it over him. It is merely a secret gloating by someone eternally under the thumb—the false sense of superiority captured so slyly by W. H. Auden's evocation of "the *Schadenfreude* / Of cooks at keyholes."

Was Nietzsche right to think of Schadenfreude as sterile and self-deluded? Might, in fact, the situation be even worse than he thought? Think of those haunted, gray-looking employees at Wernham Hogg Paper Manufacturing in the UK sitcom *The Office*. We meet them as the threat of redundancies looms, broken, depressed and frightened for their jobs. And no wonder, since their boss, David Brent, is incapable of fighting on their behalf. He lies to senior management, he boasts, he is lazy. He vainly thinks that his tasteless jokes motivate his employees (in reality his humor mostly nauseates them). But he's the boss, and so his employees play along, and register their disdain instead in their secret pleasure at his humiliations, communicated through micro-smirks and minuscule eye rolls, with smothered grins behind his back and glances at the camera; they are victims whose triumphs are only in the mind. Though David's failures will ultimately destroy them, his employees enjoy them nonetheless. These moments of one-upmanship give them a sense of superiority and control—and leave them exactly where they always were.

MIND TRICKS

Will we all suffer the same fate? Perhaps not. Bob Sutton knows all our secrets when it comes to getting payback at work. The way we steal Post-it Notes to compensate us for unpaid overtime, or come back a few minutes late from lunch—not enough so anyone would notice but enough to feel like a hero. None of these strategies will encourage an obnoxious boss to change their behavior, though they might let us feel like we run our own lives again, letting off a bit of steam and making it that little bit easier to open that spreadsheet or make that call to Bill in accounts. But could Schadenfreude ever lead to more meaningful workplace change?

If we're lucky, Schadenfreude, even of the most secret kind, might leave traces; a boss, sensing that people are laughing at her, might adjust her behavior (or else become paranoid and vindictive, so this one is a risk). Overt smirking at a new and nervous boss does seem to work in the movies. In Nancy Meyers's *What Women Want*, when their new boss Darcy (played by Helen Hunt) arrives, the macho members of the Chicago advertising firm inwardly scoff at her ideas, which simply makes her redouble her efforts and win over the team (though this may just be wishful Hollywood thinking).

Far more important is the fact that sniggering at the boss's mistakes by the water cooler or in the loo is a powerful way for employees to bond. In fact, it is so effective it is a surprise that it's not encouraged in team-building away days. And these moments of gossip might ultimately lead to some more productive conversations, such as how to gently re-educate your boss so he stops interrupting your lunch hour; or how to devise the perfectly timed revenge that makes the boss realize the error of their ways.

At the very least, Schadenfreude can provide what Bob calls a "mind trick" for surviving the daily indignities of work. Remember that dating study, in which seeing a love rival fail was thought to give students a little confidence boost — felt as Schadenfreude — which upped their own chances of success? Seeing your boss, however nice they are, accidentally locking themselves out of their office, or having a breakdown trying to unfold their brand-new, super-expensive folding bike, subtly rearranges the power balance. It might seem an inconsequential moment but, like that old sage advice to imagine your interview panel in their underwear, it might be just enough to give us the foolhardiness we need to push ourselves forward. I sheepishly tell Bob about the toilet paper on the shoe of my VC incident. That's nothing, Bob laughs. "There's a faculty member I work with who was always very horrible to me and was in a position to cause me some grief. Once I saw him give a speech — he's a famous academic — and his zipper was down. I can't even tell you how much joy I got from watching this guy speak with his fly unzipped. It still makes me so happy." Bob is laughing merrily. "I try to feel guilty about it, but I can't!"

It is ridiculous of course, but seeing those who lord it over us embarrassed, not just punished for smugness and power but exposed to be as feeble and error-prone as we feel, are tiny moments of glorious mutiny. Through them, we get a taste for recklessness and a feeling of sureness. And glimpse a world beginning to change.

8

Power

Politics, tribes, mockery

*When a British MP was caught playing Candy Crush
on his phone during a committee meeting.*

*When a former prime minister launched a "Back to
Basics" anti-sleaze campaign—and almost his entire
cabinet was forced to resign amid scandals.*

*When a Senate Commerce Committee
chairman helpfully explained that the Internet
was a "series of tubes."*

*When Barack Obama attempted to woo blue-collar voters
in Pennsylvania by going bowling, and rolled a series of
gutter balls. Later, he described his performance as "like
the Special Olympics" and had to apologize all over again.*

*When President Trump boarded Air Force One and
his comb-over was dislodged in the wind.*

On my way to work, on the morning after the American election, I joined a small crowd huddled around the news-and-sweets kiosk at the train station. It was a peculiarly old-fashioned scene, given the smartphones in our pockets. "An electrifying human drama," read one headline. "Republican takes victory on tide of popular rage," read another. Over the previous nineteen months, the soon-to-be forty-fifth president had mocked his own party grandees, taunted journalists with accusations of "fake news," and crowed with delight over the FBI investigation into his opponent's emails. Of course, Democrats were also not immune from gloating when they saw—or hoped they saw—the Republican Party in meltdown. Each revelation of misogyny, each misspelled tweet, each narcissistic rage, each glimpse of baldness proved irresistible to the makers of Internet memes, and made the likes and shares go up.

In this age of divisive politics, gloating over the catastrophes of the other side has become an all too familiar ritual. Give us a sex scandal or a hot mic gaffe, a forced resignation or PR stunt gone awry, and we will dazzle you with our wit and élan, our moral indignation amplified in the echo chambers of the Internet. The Schadenfreude we feel at a politician's mishaps is not so different from the thrill of our celebrity overlords being toppled, and is similarly concerned with entitlement to position and power. When it comes to politicians, it is their inept blunders, their moments of idiocy and, most of all, their moral hypocrisy—their insincerity and duplicity—that makes us so gleeful, providing evidence that they are not up to the job of telling us what to do.

Scoffing at the failings of the political establishment is hardly new. In 1830, when seventeen-year-old Anne Chalmers visited the

House of Commons, she described joining a group of women huddling around the ventilator above the chamber (women at that time were denied entrance to the public galleries) to hear snatches of debates float up and get a glimpse of the speakers. Two of the ladies "laughed in convulsions": "Oh! Good God! What a pair of eyes!" and "La! What frights in boots! I could speak better myself!"

Satire has played its role in democratic debate for at least two thousand years. Under many regimes, political jokes are particularly important, smuggling criticism and keeping an opposition alive. The Akan of Ghana, known for their irrepressible sense of humor, tell a joke at the expense of their corrupt local chiefs. A young man, Kwame, becomes enraged by local government corruption. But with no opportunity to confront the perpetrators, he decides to take matters into his own hands and paints a sign on his van which roughly translates as: "Some elders are darn wicked" (or probably something a bit ruder). The elders summon Kwame to the palace and order him to remove the inscription. He does. And instead writes, "Still the Same."

There are some who dismiss the subversive potential of political comedy, regarding it as a safety valve, simultaneously radical and conservative since it keeps the status quo firmly in place. Laughing might seem to lessen the anger, the urge for more meaningful action ebbing away. In our Age of Schadenfreude, sniggering at political gaffes has come in for a great deal of criticism. Some cautioned that, in the run-up to the American election, "Schadenfreude-soaked liberals," enjoying the spectacle of Republican Party infighting, were missing the severity of the threat. There is the fear that the endless clicks and shares, even if only motivated by

Schadenfreude, steal valuable column inches. Schadenfreude might exhaust itself: we will become bored. More seriously, it will stoke tribalistic resentments further. In Britain, for example, after the Brexit vote, Remainers sniggered and shared a photograph on social media of protestors standing in a roundabout holding a sign which read "Brexit Mean's Brexit" (oh, the delicious superiority of pointing out that punctuation error!). But even if this glistening triumph of Schadenfreude may be irresistible for those still coming to terms with a shock defeat, in the long term, snobbish gloating over the other side's punctuation mistakes isn't hugely constructive.

This is not the first time we have worried about the potentially corrosive effects of Schadenfreude in politics. In 1899 an ambush in the colonies by German-backed rebels resulted in the loss of several British troops. The Berlin correspondent of the *Morning Post* wrote that German journalists were being "expressly requested not to exhibit Schadenfreude at the ambush into which the British and Americans fell," for fear that they might offend the British and escalate hostilities further. The press of Leipzig, however, were later accused of losing "no opportunity of saying nasty things about our nation. Wherever we have been victorious, the publication of the official dispatch has been preceded by a leaflet handed round in the streets giving an exaggerated account of our losses." As today, Schadenfreude was cast as the moral and intellectual failing of the *other* side. And as today, Schadenfreude was feared to be so irresistible that it would make people vulnerable to misinformation—the exaggerated reports handed around on leaflets—a fake news that deepened hostilities further. Schadenfreude can be destructive in politics—although not always, as we'll discover. But more crucially: Can we really avoid it?

PARTISAN POLITICS

When young Republicans complain that
they can't get a date in Washington.

When a Tory MP called Jane Austen
"our greatest living author."

News that the new blue British passports, which
for pro-Brexit voters symbolize a return to British
independence, will be manufactured in France.

Here is a peculiar moral dilemma: the more intensely we engage with politics, and the more identified we are with a particular agenda (presumably a good thing), the more Schadenfreude we are likely to feel when the other side screws up (probably slightly less good).

In the run-up to the 2004 American presidential election, psychologists at the University of Kentucky began to investigate this link between party commitment and Schadenfreude. The participants, undergraduates at Kentucky, were assessed on the strength of their party affiliation, and later, invited to respond to a bundle of news articles. Among the reports was an article describing how, during the G8 summit in Scotland, then Republican president George W. Bush had decided to go for a cycle ride, gave a policeman a jaunty wave, then collided with him and fell off his bike.

Unsurprisingly, those who strongly identified as Democrats were most "amused" and "tickled" at the story, while Republicans reported more "concern for Bush." The participants were also given an article about Democratic challenger John Kerry photographed at the Kennedy Space Center crawling through one of the hatches of the shuttle *Discovery*, wearing a baby-blue NASA "bunny suit." (Google it: I promise it's worth it.) Overall, Republicans enjoyed Kerry's gaffe more than Democrats did.

As the 2006 midterms approached, the psychologists turned to a more hidden form of political Schadenfreude. At this time, troop deaths in Iraq were a major issue, with both sides accusing the other of "politicizing the war." The death of service people is "so manifestly negative in nature," wrote the study's authors, "that it is difficult to imagine any American citizen anywhere reporting that it could bring pleasure." However, when participants read an article about a roadside bomb in Iraq which killed a number of American personnel, some—mainly Democrats who hoped regime change at home would change the direction of foreign policy—admitted experiencing "some form of muted pleasure." "Part of me is glad as this supports my position on the war"; "happy if this helps get troops home faster." "It is important to emphasize," wrote the study's authors, who were surprised that anyone would even be willing to admit to this, "that these feelings were marked by ambivalence."

Those who expressed vindication or hopefulness about political regime change also described themselves feeling "distressed," "upset," "worried" or "sad." (This study did not adjust for age, since all respondents were in their late teens or early twenties—we might reasonably wonder how these responses change as we get older.)

In the third phase of their study, which took place during the 2008 presidential primaries, the Kentucky psychologists wanted to see if people might enjoy a political screwup *even when they themselves will suffer as a result*. Again, a pack of news articles was circulated. In it was a fictitious news story about the recession widely affecting the United States. Written by an invented high-profile economist, the article described a bill debated two years earlier. Had the bill been passed, this imaginary economist said, the banking crisis and recession would certainly have been averted. The article blamed a particular senator for casting the deciding vote against the bill. Half of the respondents read that this mis-guided person was Republican front-runner John McCain, the other half that it was Democrat Barack Obama. The article was at pains to emphasize how severe and long-lasting the recession would be, and how its effects would be felt by *all* Americans. Even in a situation where they themselves would certainly suffer, Republicans enjoyed reading that the financial crash had been caused by Obama, while Democrats reported pleasure on reading that McCain had cast the deciding vote.

Martin Amis once quipped that only British people enjoy Schadenfreude at their own expense. He was, it seems, quite wrong. What is it about the tribes we belong to that we are willing to put their interests above our own?

GROUPS

On the night Osama bin Laden was killed, large groups of Americans gathered in Times Square and outside the White House chanting "USA! USA!" Some found the celebrations deeply disturbing. The social psychologist Jonathan Haidt, writing in the *New York Times*, did not entirely agree, describing the outpouring as a moment of "collective effervescence," Émile Durkheim's term for an irrational mass euphoria, involving a loss of individuality, occasioned by some unquestionable public good.

Faced with the sometimes frightening behavior of rioting crowds or Twitter mobs, commentators have often turned to early crowd psychologists such as Gustave Le Bon and Gabriel Tarde who, in the late nineteenth and early twentieth centuries, thought a crowd robbed people of their rationality. "Crowds are not intelligent," wrote Le Bon, but rather "the sentiments and ideas of all the persons in the gathering take one and the same direction, and their conscious personality vanishes." For these historical writers, it was invariably *other people* who were most susceptible to the emotional hysteria of groups. Women, children, those described as "mentally deficient" and the "lower races" ("they," not "us") succumbed.

Most contemporary theorists of group behavior reject this approach, and certainly the racist, sexist attitudes it was embedded in. They talk not of a loss of identity when we enter a crowd, but of moving into another kind of identity, a social identity. Most of us use complex networks of social identities to position ourselves. Think of how you perceive objects in terms of categories (bicycles versus cars, for instance). The way we think of ourselves is no different, using our jobs, lifestyles, classes, football clubs and so on to situate ourselves. Such groups do not define us entirely, and few are permanent. Instead, they come in and out of focus depending on who we are talking to—when I'm talking to people who have cats, my identity as a "dog owner" may be at the forefront of my mind; when having to travel to North London, I very much regard myself as a "South Londoner."

Sociologists have studied these allegiances to "in" and "out" groups for over half a century. One of their important—and quite terrifying—insights is that it is possible to feel very strong group affiliations even when the group has been hurriedly assembled based on something as inconsequential as a coin flip or the color of someone's T-shirt. This finding, known as the "minimal group paradigm," was first described by H. Tajfel and his colleagues in the 1970s. It shows that we need not share any values or opinions at all to form a group and defend it vigorously—but that these may well align later.

Their other key insight is that once in/out groups are established, rivalries set in very quickly. We are more likely to show favoritism toward our in-groups and bias against out-groups. More likely to see members of our in-group as individuals with deep and complex inner lives, while seeing members of out-groups as less intelligent and less autonomous than us. Most of all, we are so eager to protect the reputations of our in-groups, that we tend to exaggerate our own group's success and derogate, and rejoice in, the failures of the out-group. In other words, when we form ourselves into groups we are much more likely to indulge in Schadenfreude. And we are also less afraid to show it. Groups embolden us, and give us anonymity and backup if things go wrong; the gloating and taunting you'd be nervous to do alone if you happened to meet a supporter of your rival football team in a dark alley become much easier when you can feel a crowd at your back—or on your Twitter feed.

The effects of in/out group behavior are all around us—in the rivalries between local scout clubs, in the way we think about which "zone" to sit in in our open-plan office at work. And of course, it is there in politics. "We can control the Schadenfreude," says C. J. in *The West Wing* after Josh is embroiled in a scandal, "make sure he's still standing in a week." "Schadenfreude?" asks Donna. "You know," says C. J., "enjoying the suffering of others, the whole rationale behind the House of Representatives."

One effect of Schadenfreude is that it brings a feeling of temporary—and often unearned—glory, since, as with sports, a rival's mistake may well translate into an advantage for you. Another is that we are very eager to share news of our rival's failures, which then strengthens—and sometimes broadens—our group affiliations further. Psychologists have even observed this effect in something as trivial as the phone in our pockets. In one study, BlackBerry users were given a story about a bug that was plaguing Apple's iPhone. Not only did BlackBerry users feel high levels of Schadenfreude on reading the story, they also eagerly shared the news with their BlackBerry-owning friends, strengthening their own and other people's allegiances to the in-group by relishing the thought of Apple users—who they also perceived as smug and self-important—being frustrated and miserable.

Humans are nothing if not amusingly lacking in self-awareness.

Though we are highly likely to feel Schadenfreude toward the "out-group," we are also more likely to attribute Schadenfreude to them too—since we habitually see Schadenfreude as a failing, evidence of being overly emotional and easily swayed, and a mere compensation for being the underdog who must resort to sniggering in the absence of genuine power. In a divisive political landscape, Republicans accuse Democrats of Schadenfreude; Democrats, Republicans.

But strip Schadenfreude of its moral associations, and it emerges as neither good nor bad, but as a behavior which will inevitably emerge when we form ourselves into groups. It mobilizes and strengthens our tribe. It gives a feeling of swagger, a taste of glory. It creates political momentum. And, of course, this is precisely why it can be used so knowingly and so effectively.

TINY REVOLUTIONS

The power of Schadenfreude has long been known by feminist campaigners—which is satisfying, since Schadenfreude has historically been judged a peculiarly female moral failing. Kant in the eighteenth and Schopenhauer in the nineteenth century both associated sniggering at other people's downfalls with those other womanly vices—gossip, manipulation and lying. For Max Scheler, Schadenfreude was inevitably a feature of female psychology, since "she is the weaker and therefore the more vindictive sex." In fact, recent research suggests that men experience more frequent and intense Schadenfreude (though such statistics may be skewed by the fact that women may feel more awkward admitting their pleasure at other people's misery, since it clashes so much with the social imperative that women be nice).

In the late nineteenth and early twentieth centuries, however, suffragettes and suffragists in Britain and America reclaimed Schadenfreude as their own, and used it to undermine their opponents. The dominant culture had ridiculed the suffragettes. There were picture postcards depicting emasculated husbands poorly attempting to serve up dinner. There were journalists who described the mass and often violent arrests of suffragettes as reminding them "very much of the removal of naughty kittens."

The campaigners for women's votes found ways to turn the mockery back on their opponents. At their open-air rallies, they made hecklers victims of witty backchat, redirecting the crowd's ridicule toward their opponents. The English suffragette Annie Kenney, one of the working-class women in the movement, recalled a rally in Somerset, where every few minutes an elderly man shouted: "If you were my wife I'd give you poison." Eventually the speaker replied, "Yes, and if I were your wife I'd take it."

And then there were the guerrilla tactics which made their political rivals appear ludicrous. Cabinet ministers routinely avoided being heckled by suffragettes by refusing to speak at public meetings when women were in the audiences. In response, suffragettes learned to sneak into halls in advance, in several cases hiding under the organ. When the talk began, they began to speak too, their voices floating out of the pipes and confounding the stewards, making the audience snigger and leaving the ministers ruffled and confused, impossible to take seriously. These moments of glorious anarchy certainly weren't the only approach being used by campaigners, and wouldn't be enough to spark political change on their own. But they could momentarily upset the usual power relations, and create a sense of possibility and camaraderie. "Every joke," as George Orwell said, "is a tiny revolution."

Mockery and contempt remain a crucial part of feminist activism, scrappy tactics to expose hidden forms of discrimination. In 2012, then governor of Massachusetts Mitt Romney was asked about pay equality and hiring in a presidential debate. His now infamous response? He breezily explained that his staff had brought him "whole binders full of women." Before the debate was even over, a Twitter account @Romneys_Binder (portraying itself as a binder) had attracted 14,000 followers, and there was a Tumblr page filled with mocking gifs—mainly stock photos of women with binders. Within a day, there were blogs, tweets and a Facebook page about "Binders Full of Women," which had received 274,000 likes. Amazon users posted satirical reviews of binders, with other users declaring the responses "helpful" to bump them up: "Outwardly these would make the ideal binder in which to keep women—brightly colored, sassy, and individual with a modern feel! Sadly however they're still too small...legs, arms and heads still protruded."

Another chimed in, "You have no idea how frustrating it is, trying to find a binder that can contain all my various women...If you're a guy looking to contain a whole lot of women (of any size), this is the binder for you!"

And another: "While these binders are well made, attractive and reasonably priced, they are unfortunately too small to put women in."

And another: "Maybe it's just my women, but they don't seem to want to fit into the space I've designated for them in this binder."

These virtuoso displays of mockery, these pile-ons, have become an almost predictable feature of our political landscape—part of what might lead us to think of ours as an Age of Schadenfreude. The question is: Will they keep working? Or has our eagerness to leap on another's disgrace become a mere habit, an unthinking reflex?

What might work well when it punches up to the privileged is less appealing when it is striking out in every direction—left, right and down to the less fortunate. The more habitual Schadenfreude seems, the more nervous we become about its capacity to silence, to eliminate dissent and to inhibit constructive debate, and also to reinforce those polarized camps, in which moral indignation simply ricochets, with occasional insults lobbed across the divide.

We may reasonably fear that living in an Age of Schadenfreude puts people off public life, and cheapens the discourse. We may also quite reasonably fear that Schadenfreude will lose its frisson of rebellion and giddy defiance that once gave it its luster, and that indulging our taste for other people's gaffes will become merely cruel and excessive, an unpleasant end in itself.

Yet, isn't it precisely this risk that Schadenfreude can and does go too far—that it becomes compromised, or feels confusing or unhelpful—that keeps us interested in it? We may fear we are blindly, blithely indulging our taste for other people's disasters. Yet it is easy to forget that moral confusion is part of how we experience Schadenfreude too — that nagging worry that we won't know when we've reached the line and will just keep going.

Stand-up comics recognize, and tease us with, such moments of moral confusion. Laughter might seem anarchic, but it also creates conformity. At a stand-up gig, audience members may find themselves laughing along with a joke, only to regret laughing later. Other times, we may realize that everyone else has stopped laughing and we will clam up too, not wanting to be exposed or assent to some horrifying proposition. These moments confront us with how easily we join in with Schadenfreude. But they also remind us that flirting with the morally questionable, testing the limits of where we "ought" to stop, is an exciting game. And is especially provocative when it comes to liberal audiences, who may see themselves as more empathic and compassionate, for whom laughing at other people's painful humiliations — or just their pain, however deserved — might create an extra layer of social discomfort.

So will we know when to stop? Remember Homer Simpson's amusing fantasy about his smug neighbor meeting a series of catastrophes, which suddenly turns unfunny when a scene of the neighbor's funeral pops into Homer's head? At what point does your conscience intervene and make your delightfully frothy Schadenfreude curdle and split? At what point do you say "too much"? When a worthy environmentalist MP is discovered clearing ancient woodland to make room for his fancy new extension — and receives a catastrophic public shaming on Twitter? When a politician who lied about a parking ticket is sent to prison? When someone who has expressed views you find obnoxious and reprehensible meets some freak accident (crashing his light aircraft, for instance)?

At the beginning of her 2016 show *Stand Up for Her*, Bridget Christie tells us a true story about Formula One motor-racing legend Sir Stirling Moss. In an interview for BBC Radio, Moss had said that he was "not surprised" that there were so few women in F1.

"I think they have the strength, but I don't know if they've got the mental aptitude to race," he said.

What Christie tells us next may please you:

Moss walked into an empty lift shaft, fell and broke his ankles.

Did you smile?

Schadenfreude:
The Rules of Engagement

I had hoped for a happy ending. Something like (clears throat): In writing this book, I have been on a voyage of discovery. I have tamed my Schadenfreude. I feel appropriate empathy for the suffering of pop stars/models/politicians. I have stopped watching fail videos. And when my friends do something better than me, and it doesn't quite come off in the way they hoped, I no longer detect a faint echo of relief. I am, in short, a better person.

But you know already that's not true.

If anything, the opposite has happened. Studying this emotion has made me more attuned to it. I have a little twinge of excitement at someone else's misery, and I try to catch it like a spider under a glass to peer at it more closely. I have become something of a connoisseur of Schadenfreude, with a fine nose for its subtle, ever-changing palate, savoring its movements from glee to triumph, from quiet satisfaction to smugness and contempt—before settling, inevitably, into that familiar sour aftertaste of self-disgust.

Perhaps now that you've got to the end of this book, you are also feeling a little queasy at realizing just how large a role enjoying other people's misfortunes plays in all our lives. Perhaps you are feeling a bit exposed too, and unsure. You'd very much like me to offer you some consoling final thoughts. What, if anything, ought one to do with all this Schadenfreude?

I can certainly sympathize. I'm always grateful to find something vaguely useful at the end of a book like this, a party bag of tools for tinkering with some rusty corner of my life.

Of course, I'm not a psychologist or a moralist, and I'm certainly not a self-help guru. But truth is, in the time I've spent thinking about this most ethically ambiguous of emotions, I have, more or less, made my peace with it. And so here I've tried to break down my new relationship with Schadenfreude into a few basic principles; some Rules of Engagement, if you like:

1. SCHADENFREUDE HELPS

Do you instinctively think Schadenfreude is a "bad" emotion, something pinched and sly, something to feel a little guilty about?

I don't think Schadenfreude is either "good" or "evil": sometimes it stirs up problems, but mostly it's harmless fun. But let's focus on its benefits, and there are many: it makes you feel good when you are feeling inferior; it is a way of celebrating the fact that everyone fails; it helps us see the absurdity in life; it can spark a rebellious streak, or provide the little jolt of superiority that might give us the boldness to push ourselves forward; it can even help change conversations at a political level. Schadenfreude might seem a negative, mean-spirited and self-defeating emotion, and while it can be all of those things, it can be rather useful too.

2. SCHADENFREUDE WON'T DEFINE YOU

Do you worry that a shiver of pleasure at a friend's bad news somehow wipes out the compassion you also feel? Do you fear that you might be that worst of all things: a hypocrite?

Most people who have spent time thinking about Schadenfreude agree that it is possible to feel an unexpected twinge of pleasure at the same time as experiencing very genuine feelings of concern and sympathy. It is perfectly possible to find yourself suppressing a sudden desire to laugh at the same time as wanting to console. Or to feel a surge of relief while also experiencing an echo of the loss our friend feels. This is our extraordinary capacity as humans, a level of emotional flexibility which is so much more interesting than moral rigidity—and more truthful too. It is something to be proud of.

3. SCHADENFREUDE TELLS YOU THINGS YOU DON'T WANT TO KNOW

Could you spot your Schadenfreude at twenty paces? Would you be able to identify the subtle differences between its tastes and textures? Being able to recognize the fine differences in our emotional weather is an important part of emotional intelligence, and particularly valuable when it comes to those feelings we habitually ignore because they make us feel ashamed of ourselves.

Schadenfreude happens for a reason. And when we are willing to look it in the eye, it's easier to ask what prompted it in the first place. Did you think the person deserved a comeuppance? Why? Was your pleasure more about winning? And if so, against whom? Do you envy the person whose suffering you are enjoying? Were they making you feel inadequate or vulnerable? Betrayed? Misrepresented? Angry?

Noticing our Schadenfreude and understanding why it feels so deliciously satisfying can help us face up to the more excruciating feelings underneath.

4. OWN UP TO YOUR SCHADENFREUDE (SOMETIMES)

This seems a ludicrously risky strategy, but bear with me. It's unlikely to go brilliantly if you admit your Schadenfreude to your boss, or to your paranoid cousin. And no one likes people who go around openly smirking at other people's bad news. (At least have the grace to try to hide it!)

Every so often, though, we all feel a moment of Schadenfreude that jars, and makes us uncomfortable. And when this happens—and the person in question is someone you trust—the best option may be to find a way to tell them.

Philippa Perry suggests opening the conversation with something like this: "I noticed I felt superior when you didn't get that new job . . . I thought that was inappropriate, and I wonder if you have similar feelings, for instance, when I couldn't afford a new car but you could?"

I tried something like this at home. While I was writing this book, my husband was also writing one, which he finished before me. And to make matters worse, he got an admiring and congratulatory email from his editor *on the same day* I received yet another "So, er, where is it?" email from mine.

So when my husband came home that night, a little bit of me *really* wanted to hear that between the lines of the email he'd received was a big list of problems with the book. And how it would take my husband many months to slog through them all. And how demoralized he felt. Actually, what happened is that he pootled off to make himself a celebratory cup of tea and then we had a big fight about whose job it had been to pay the council tax. (I still maintain it was his.)

Later on, when the dust had settled, I confessed that alongside feeling pleased about the email, I had also felt rise up in me a desire for it to have gone less well — and now I was feeling pretty ashamed.

Since my husband is a very kind person, he laughed. And then we bonded over how much we both hate this horribly successful writer whose sneery review we'd just read in the paper.

And so, despite all expectations, confessing did make me feel better.

5. SCHADENFREUDE GOES BOTH WAYS

Last, and most importantly: What should we do when we see someone attempting to suppress a delicious twinge of satisfaction at our own great failure? Well, obviously, that is outrageous, and you should revoke your friendship with them immediately. But failing that, what else could you do?

First, don't point it out; that's just mean. It's one thing acknowledging your own shabby Schadenfreude, quite another to embarrass other people.

But admit yours straight back if they've been brave enough to admit theirs.

Finally, feel smug (but not too smug). If you are the victim of someone else's Schadenfreude, you are seen as a worthy opponent. You have — or had, but don't worry, you'll get it again — something they want. Think back to those times when you've enjoyed their losses. Unless you very much deserve your misery (in which case, take a long hard look at yourself), their glee will tell you a lot about how inadequate you've made them feel. And this is a kind of gift, a moment of solace amid your moment of terrible angst and failure.

It can sometimes feel as if we live in a world bent on chasing perfection, a world where our faults are something to be disciplined and ideally eradicated altogether. Looking more closely at Schadenfreude tells a different story, of the joy and relief that can be found in other people's mistakes — as well as our own.

Schadenfreude might seem malicious, but when we look more closely, a far more complex emotional landscape emerges. A superior smirk is revealed as a sign of vulnerability. What might seem a sort of hate may really be a conflicted kind of love and a desire to belong. What perks us up when we hear news of someone else's misfortune is the discovery that we are not alone in our disappointments, but are part of a community of the failed.

Schadenfreude might be a flaw, granted. But we need it.

It is probably not too much to call it a salvation.

Acknowledgments

Thank you most of all to my wonderful editors Kirty Topiwala and Tracy Behar, and to Andrew Franklin, Cecily Gayford, Penny Daniel and everyone on the teams at Profile Books, Little, Brown and Wellcome Collection (especially Suzanne Connelly). Thank you to Jon Elek and Rosa Schierenberg at United Agents.

This book was written as part of my research fellowship with the "Living With Feeling" project at the Queen Mary University of London's Centre for the History of the Emotions. Thank you to Wellcome, which funded this project, and to all involved with the Centre, most of all Thomas Dixon for his unfailing support and encouragement.

Special thanks go to all those who agreed to be interviewed for this book: Caspar Addyman, James Kimmel Jr., Lisa Feldman Barrett, John Portmann, Philippa Perry and Robert I. Sutton. Thank you for your time and humor.

I am especially grateful to the following people, who generously shared their thoughts and expertise: Richard H. Smith, Molly Crockett, Elsa Richardson, Richelle Whitehead, Kirsty Leanne Kynaston Gardiner, Jules Evans and Rob Briner. There are many others, too numerous to mention here, who offered suggestions and confessed their secret Schadenfreude along the way — thank you! I am, as always, indebted to my brilliant colleagues in the Queen Mary University of London School of English and Drama.

Thank you to David McFetridge, Catherine Nixey, Tom Whipple and Jo Fidgen for your pro tips.

And as always, thank you to my family — especially to Tom, Enda and Dermot for your Schadenfreude anecdotes, to Carmel for so much support of many kinds, and to my parents, Ian and Ursula, for their unfailing generosity and help. Thank you Alice and Edward for so much delight. And most of all, thank you to Michael Hughes, whose encouragement, example and love make this possible at all.

Referenced Works

p. vii, "The blessed in the kingdom": Thomas Aquinas, *Summa Theologiae*, III, Supplementum, Q.94, Article 1.

A COMMUNITY OF THE FAILED

p. 2, "To see others suffer does one good": Friedrich Nietzsche, *On The Genealogy of Morality* (1887), trans. Carol Diethe, Cambridge, Cambridge University Press, 1997, pp. 42–3.

p. 2, "For the Melanesians who live on the remote Nissan Atoll": Steven R. Nachman, "Discomforting Laughter: 'Schadenfreude' among Melanesians," *Journal of Anthropological Research*, vol. 42, no. 1, Spring 1986, pp. 53–67.

p. 3, "in a laboratory in Würzburg in Germany in 2015": L. Boecker et al., "The face of schadenfreude: Differentiation of joy and schadenfreude by electromyography," *Cognitive Emotion*, vol. 29(6), 2015, pp. 1,117–25.

p. 4, "want names": Thomas Hobbes, "Human Nature" (1640), in *Human Nature and De Corpore Politico*, Oxford, Oxford University Press, 2008, pp. 21–108, 58.

p. 4, "there is no English word for Schadenfreude": quoted in Wilco W. van Dijk and Jaap W. Ouwerkerk (eds), *Schadenfreude: Understanding Pleasure at the Misfortune of Others*, Cambridge, Cambridge University Press, 2014, p. 2.

p. 6, "an infallible sign of a thoroughly bad heart": Arthur Schopenhauer, *On the Basis of Morality* (1841), trans. E. F. J. Payne, Indianapolis, Bobbs-Merrill, 1965, p. 135.

p. 7, "For Trench, the mere existence": Richard Chenevix Trench, *On the Study of Words*, London and New York, Macmillan, 1872, p. 68.

p. 8, "a secret satisfaction, of the malicious": Thomas Carlyle, "Shooting Niagara: And After?" (1867), in *The Works of Thomas Carlyle, Vol. 30, Critical and Miscellaneous*, vol. 6, Cambridge, Cambridge University Press, 2010, p. 11, 1–48.

p. 8, "indulge in what the Germans call "Schadenfreude": "Chess," *The Hull Packet and East Riding Times*, 27 May 1881.

p. 8, "In the 1890s, animal-rights campaigner": Frances Power Cobbe, "Schadenfreude" (1902), in *Prose by Victorian Women: An Anthology*, Andrea Broomfield and Sally Mitchell (eds), Abingdon, Routledge, 1996, pp. 335–50.

p. 8, "a certain amount of what the Germans call Schadenfreude": The physician Sir William Gull, "Our London Letter," *The Sheffield and Rotherham Independent*, 19 October 1887.

p. 9, "I thank God, I thank God": William Shakespeare, *The Merchant of Venice*, III:i, pp. 95–7.

p. 10, "the revenge of the impotent": Friedrich Nietzsche, *On the Genealogy of Morality*, p. 20.

p. 11, "Golden Age of Schadenfreude": https://afterdeadline.blogs.nytimes.com/2009/01/13/the-age-of-schadenfreude/.

p. 12, "We are living in an Age of Schadenfreude": https://www.theguardian.com/commentisfree/2017/may/02/fyre-festival-brexit-schadenfreude-emotion-defines-times.

p. 13, "the chronic malady of our times": Charles Dickens, *Bleak House* (1853), Oxford, Oxford University Press, 1948, p. 9.

p. 13, "When the BBC reported the robbery": http://www.bbc.co.uk/news/world-europe-37546307.

p. 15, "The Germans have a word for this": Simon Baron-Cohen, *Zero Degrees of Empathy: A New Theory of Human Cruelty*, London, Allen Lane, 2012, p. 64.

p. 15, "that strange sense of inner satisfaction": Fyodor Dostoevsky, *Crime and Punishment* (1866), trans. Nicolas Pasternak Slater, Oxford, Oxford University Press, 2017, p. 161.

1: ACCIDENTS

p. 22, "In the third century AD, the emperor Elagabalus": This anecdote appears in Mary Beard, *Laughter in Ancient Rome: On Joking, Tickling and Cracking Up*, Oakland, University of California Press, 2014, p. 77.

p. 22, "There is an ancient Egyptian tomb": Salvatore Attardo (ed), *Encyclopedia of Humor Studies*, LA and London, Sage, 2014, p. 28.

p. 22, "In 2011, a group of evolutionary psychologists": R. I. M. Dunbar et al., "Social laughter is correlated with an elevated pain threshold," *Proceedings of the Royal Society B*, vol. 279, 2012, p. 1,731. The anecdote about Mr. Bean appears in Dunbar's interview with the BBC. http://www.bbc.co.uk/news/science-environment-14889165.

Referenced works

p. 23, "the Sanskrit poet Bhanu Datta": Salvatore Attardo (ed), *Encyclopedia of Humor Studies*, LA and London, Sage, 2014, p. 657.

p. 24, "the Warlpiri of Yuendumu, in central Australia": Y. Musharbash, "Perilous Laughter: Examples from Yuendumu, Central Australia," *Anthropological Forum*, vol. 18(3), 2008, pp. 271–7.

p. 25, "Freud has this theory": Sigmund Freud, *The Joke and Its Relation to the Unconscious* (1905), London, Penguin, 2002, p. 218.

p. 28, "He called it 'Ilinx' ": Roger Caillois, *Man, Play and Games* (1958), trans. Meyer Barash, New York, Free Press, 2001, p. 24.

p. 28, "Amusingly / Robbed of his umbrella": Salvatore Attardo (ed), *Encyclopedia of Humor Studies*, LA and London, Sage, 2014, p. 678.

p. 28, "picture to yourself certain characters": Henri Bergson, *Laughter: An Essay on the Meaning of the Comic* (1900), trans. Cloudesley Brereton and Fred Rothwell, New York, Dover, 2005, p. 46.

p. 29, "The Earle of Oxford": John Aubrey, *Brief Lives* (written 1679–80), London, Vintage, 2016, p. 305

p. 29, "Driving back after a lovely meal": "Are these the worst dates you've ever heard?." https://www.bbc.co.uk/news/uk-england-41173459

2: GLORY

p. 36, "There is the satisfaction": Susan Sontag, *Regarding the Pain of Others*, London, Hamish Hamilton, 2003, p. 37.

p. 36, " 'Laughter,' he wrote 'is nothing else but a sudden glory' ": Thomas Hobbes, *Human Nature*, p. 54.

p. 36, "In 1727, John Byron, navy officer": repr. in Travis Elborough and Nick Rennison (eds), *A London Year: Daily Life in the Capital in Diaries, Journals and Letters*, London, Frances Lincoln, 2013.

p. 37, "In *The Republic*, written in the fourth century BC": Plato, *The Republic*, trans. D. Lee, Harmondsworth, Penguin, 1988, pp. 215–16.

p. 37, "I have heard of men who have travelled": Charles Maturin, *Melmoth the Wanderer* (1820), Oxford, Oxford University Press, 2008, p. 203.

p. 38, "How sweet it is to watch from dry land": Lucretius, *The Nature of Things*, trans. A. E. Stallings, London, Penguin, 2007, p. 36.

p. 38, "*The Storm* (1755)": Quoted in Carl Thompson (ed), *Shipwreck in Art and Literature: Images and Interpretations from Antiquity to the Present Day*, Abingdon, Routledge, 2013, p. 115.

p. 39, "delightful horror": Edmund Burke, *A Philosophical Enquiry into the Sublime and Beautiful* (1757), London and New York, Routledge, 2008, p. 134.

p. 39, "the eighteenth-century art theorist Jean-Baptiste Dubos": Jean-Baptiste Dubos, *Critical Reflections on Poetry, Painting and Music* (1719), trans. Thomas Nugent, London, Nourse, 1748.

p. 39, "If evolution and the survival of the fittest be true at all": William James, *The Principles of Psychology* (1890), London, Macmillan, 1891, pp. 412–13.

p. 40, "the chase / and the escape, the error": William Carlos Williams, "The crowd at the ball game" (1923), in *William Carlos Williams: Selected Poems*, London, Penguin, 1976, p. 58.

p. 41, "During the 2010 World Cup, two Dutch psychologists": J. W. Ouwerkerk, and W. W. van Dijk (eds), "Intergroup Rivalry and Schadenfreude," in *Schadenfreude: Understanding Pleasure at the Misfortunes of Others*, 2014, pp. 186–99, 186–7.

p. 43, "people in the restaurant roared with delight": The Fifth Down, *New York Times* NFL Blog, https://fifthdown.blogs.nytimes.com/2008/09/08/manhattan-cheered-bradys-injury-did-you/.

3: JUSTICE

p. 45, "Send prayers & good wishes," Lisa Coen, 6 August, 2017

p. 48, "loathsome": Søren Kierkegaard, *Works of Love* (1847), trans. H. V. Hong and E. H. Hong, New Jersey, Princeton University Press, 1995, p. 257.

p. 48, "what clearer sign of debility could there be": Charles Baudelaire, "Of the Essence of Laughter" (1855), in *Baudelaire: Selected Writings on Art and Literature*, trans. P. E. Charvet, London, Penguin, 2006, pp. 140–64, 146.

p. 48, "When someone who delights in annoying": Immanuel Kant, *Critique of Practical Reason* (1788), trans. Lewis White Beck, Chicago, University of Chicago Press, 1949, p. 170.

p. 51, "The study, carried out by Swiss researchers in 2004": Dominique J. F. de Quervain et al., "The Neural Basis of Altruistic Punishment," *Science*, 27 August 2004, pp. 305, 1,254–8.

p. 51, "during experiments like the one described above": Ernst Fehr and Simon Gächter, "Altruistic Punishment in Humans," *Nature*, vol. 415, January 2002, pp. 139–40.

p. 51, "A more recent study has suggested": M. J. Crockett et al., "The Value of Vengeance and the Demand for Deterrence," *Journal of Experimental Psychology*, vol. 143(6), 2014, pp. 2,279–86.

p. 52, "A group of researchers in Leipzig set up a puppet theater": Natacha Mendes et al., "Preschool children and chimpanzees incur costs to watch punishment of antisocial others," *Nature Human Behaviour*, vol. 2, 2018, pp. 45–51.

p. 52, "He points to a study": A. Strobel et al., "Beyond Revenge: Neural and Genetic Bases of Altruistic Punishment," *NeuroImage*, vol. 54(1), 2011, pp. 671–80.

p. 52, "and another that shows": Tania Singer et al., "Empathic Neural Responses are Modulated by the Perceived Fairness of Others," *Nature*, 2006, pp. 439, 466–9.

p. 52, "There is even a study that suggests that pleasure peaks": K. M. Carlsmith et al., "The paradoxical consequences of revenge," *Journal of Personality and Social Psychology*, vol. 95(6), pp. 1,316–24.

p. 54, "an initial happy little 'Oh, wow, someone is *fucked*' ": Jon Ronson, *So You've Been Publically Shamed*, London, Picador, 2016, p. 68.

p. 54, "The cultural theorist Adam Kotsko": Adam Kotsko, *Awkwardness: An Essay*, Washington, O Books, 2010.

p. 56, "what Lisa calls our own 'affective niche' ": Lisa Feldman Barrett, *How Emotions Are Made: The Secret Life of the Brain*, London, Macmillan, 2017, p. 73.

4: THE SMUG

p. 61, "You're not to think you *are* anything special": Aksel Sandemose, *A Fugitive Crosses His Tracks* (1933), New York, Knopf, 1936, pp. 77–8.

p. 62, "much laughinge of the standers by": Baldassare Castiglione, *The Book of the Courtier* (1528/1561 trans.), London, J. M. Dent, 1994, p. 43.

p. 62, "Among the Torres Strait Islanders": J. Beckett, "Laughing with, Laughing at, among Torres Strait Islanders," *Anthropological Forum*, vol. 18(3), 2008, pp. 295–302.

p. 64, "utmost enjoyment of spoiling a friend's self-satisfaction": George Eliot, "The Sad Fortunes of the Reverend Amos Barton," in *Scenes of Clerical Life* (1857), Oxford, OUP, 2015, pp. 3–70, 7.

p. 66, "laden with years, and lingering away": Jean de La Fontaine, *The Fables of La Fontaine* (1668–1694), trans. R. Thomson, Edinburgh and London, Ballantyne, 1884, p. 71.

p. 68, "covered in shame": Alexander Roberts and James Donaldson (eds), *The Writings of Quintus Sept. Flor. Tertullianus, vol. 1*, Edinburgh, Clark, 1870, p. 34.

p. 69, "day of national humiliation": Abraham Lincoln, "Proclamation 97: Appointing a Day of National Humiliation, Fasting and Prayer," 30 March 1863.

p. 69, "the biggest failure I knew": J. K. Rowling, Commencement Address, Harvard University, 5 June 2008.

p. 72, "Tigger is getting so bouncy nowadays": A. A. Milne, *The World of Pooh*, Toronto, McClelland, 1977, p. 251.

5: Love

p. 78, "do not triumph in your brother's disgrace": Felix Adler, *Moral Instruction of Children* (1893), New York, Appleton, 1905, p. 212.

p. 79, "maintain a conventional air of distress": Iris Murdoch, *A Severed Head*, London, Vintage, 2001, p. 33.

p. 81, "When psychologists asked in one study": S. J. Solnick and D. Hemenway, "Is More Always Better?," *Journal of Economic Behavior & Organization*, vol. 37, 1998, pp. 373–83.

p. 84, "The hypothesis was simple": L. Colyn and A. Gordon, "Schadenfreude as a mate-value-tracking mechanism," *Personal Relationships*, vol. 20(3), September 2013, p. 20.

p. 85, "During the Second World War": Samuel Stouffer et al., *The American Soldier: Adjustment to Army Life, vol. 1.*, New Jersey, Princeton University Press, 1949.

p. 86, "A house may be large or small": Karl Marx, "Wage-Labour and Capital" (1847), repr. in David McLellan (ed), *Karl Marx: Selected Writings*, Oxford, Oxford University Press, 2000, p. 284.

p. 86, "In the 1980s the psychologist Tom Wills": T. A. Wills, "Downward comparison principles in social psychology," *Psychological Bulletin*, vol. 90, 1981, pp. 245–71.

p. 87, "Taylor noticed that during their interviews": J. V. Wood, S. E. Taylor and R. Lichtman, "Social comparison in adjustment to breast cancer," *Journal of Personality and Social Psychology*, vol. 49, 1985, pp. 1,169–83.

p. 87, "More recent research": B. Buunk et al., "The affective consequences of social comparison: either direction has its ups and downs," *Journal of Personality and Social Psychology*, vol. 59, 1990, pp. 1,238–49.

p. 90, "In the late 2000s, a choir was set up in Durban": S. P. Black, "Laughing to Death: Joking as Support amid Stigma for Zulu-speaking South Africans Living with HIV," *Journal of Linguistic Anthropology*, 22 January 2012, pp. 87–108.

p. 90, "While she was living among the Makushi": L. Scherberger, "The janus-faced shaman: the role of laughter in sickness and healing among the Makushi," *Anthropology and Humanism*, 30 January 2005, pp. 55–69.

6: Envy

p. 95, "an absolute running of two souls into one": Ralph Waldo Emerson, *Essays: First Series* (1841), Boston, Munroe, 1850, p. 190.

p. 95, "If you have either no fellow-feeling": Adam Smith, *The Theory of Moral Sentiments* (1759), London, Millar, 1761, p. 26.

p. 96, "in the adversity of our best friends": François de La Rochefoucauld, *Collected Maxims and Other Reflections* (1664), Maxim 1:99, Oxford, Oxford University Press, 2007, p. 155.

p. 99, "he doth bestride the narrow world": William Shakespeare, *Julius Caesar*, I:ii, pp. 135–8.

p. 101, "on three or four occasions": quoted in John L. Locke, *Eavesdropping: An Intimate History*, Oxford, Oxford University Press, 2010, p. 164.

p. 104, "You're a creature of 'contempt and malice'": Clifford Odets and Ernest Lehman, *Sweet Smell of Success*, dir. Alexander Mackendrick, 1957.

7: MUTINY

p. 114, "There was the radio producer...the CEO...the corporate lawyer's secretary": Robert I. Sutton, *The No Asshole Rule*, London, Sphere, 2010, pp. 32–3, 130.

p. 117, "His soul *squints*": Friedrich Nietzsche, *On the Genealogy of Morality*, pp. 20–1.

p. 117, "I don't know when I've had a more juicy moment": P. G. Wodehouse, "The inimitable Jeeves" (1923), in *The Jeeves Omnibus*, vol. 1, London, Hutchinson, 2006, pp. 401–580, 432.

p. 118, "the *Schadenfreude* / Of cooks at keyholes": W. H. Auden, *The Age of Anxiety* (1947), Princeton, Princeton University Press, 2011, p. 6.

8: POWER

p. 123, "laughed in convulsions": Anne Chalmers, *The Letters and Journals of Anne Chalmers* (1830), London, Chelsea, 1923, p. 95.

p. 123, "The Akan of Ghana": S. Attardo (ed), *Encyclopedia of Humor Studies*, vol. 1, p. 21.

p. 123, "Schadenfreude-soaked liberals": Isaac Chotiner, "Against Liberal Schadenfreude," *Slate Magazine*, 12 March 2016.

p. 124, "expressly requested not to exhibit Schadenfreude": "The Samoan Difficulty," *The Morning Post*, 13 April 1899.

p. 124, "no opportunity of saying nasty things": "German Unfriendliness," *The North-Eastern Daily Gazette*, 20 February 1900.

Referenced works

p. 125, "In the run-up to the 2004 American presidential election": David J. Y. Combs, Caitlin A. J. Powell, David Ryan Schurtz and Richard H. Smith, "Politics, *schadenfreude* and ingroup identification: The sometimes happy thing about a poor economy and death," *Journal of Experimental Social Psychology*, vol. 45, 2009, pp. 635–46.

p. 128, "collective effervescence": Jonathan Haidt, "Why We Celebrate a Killing," *New York Times*, 7 May 2011.

p. 129, "minimal group paradigm": H. Tajfel, "Experiments in intergroup discrimination," *Scientific American*, vol. 223, 1970, pp. 96–102.

p. 130, "We can control the Schadenfreude": *The West Wing*, "Disaster Relief," season 5, episode 6, NBC, created by Aaron Sorkin, 5 November 2003.

p. 130, "In one study, BlackBerry users": J. W. Ouwerkerk et al., "When we enjoy bad news about other groups: A social identity approach to out-group Schadenfreude," in *Group Processes and Intergroup Relations*, vol. 21.1, 2018, pp. 214–32.

p. 131, "she is the weaker and therefore the more vindictive sex": Max Scheler, *Ressentiment* (1915), Milwaukee, Marquette, 1994, p. 15.

p. 132, "very much of the removal of naughty kittens": *Daily Express*, 21 March 1907.

p. 132, "If you were my wife I'd give you poison": quoted in Krista Cowman, "'Doing Something Silly': The uses of humour by the Women's Social and Political Union, 1903–1914," *International Review of Social History*, vol. 52, 2007, pp. 259–74, 268.

p. 133, "Every joke": George Orwell, "Funny, But Not Vulgar" (1944), repr. in *George Orwell, As I Please*, S. Orwell and Ian Angus (eds), D. R. Godine, 1968, p. 184.

An Index of Schadenfreude

A select catalog of its variations,
causes and consequences

Accidents
  involving
    bees, 21
    ice, 19–20, 39, 40
    puddles, 28
    wind, 28
  suffered by
    cats, 16, 69
    keep-fit enthusiasts, 20
Awkward feeling, following
    misjudged Schadenfreude,
    10–11, 32, 54, 126–7
    (see also: Shame)

Bosses, bad, 113–20
  away days, 119
  flies (undone), 120
  laxatives, 114
  meetings, 111

Cackling, villainous, 9
Celebrities, 100–5
  arrested, 100
  dumped, 1
  in diet failure, 2

Dates, bad, 29–30, 35, 79, 84
"Delightful horror," pleasant
    shuddering, etc., 35–8

Enhanced sex-appeal, as not
    unpleasant side-effect
    of Schadenfreude,
    79–80

Fantasy comeuppances, of
    exes, 16, 70.
    geography teachers, 72
    queue-jumpers, 45

Farts, relating to, 5–6, 20, 29, 91
Ferocious thrill, 8, 39, 127

Giddy, following glass breaking,
        explosions, etc., 27–8
Gloating, 25, 49, 62, 78, 122
    at safe distance, 3, 9, 117,
        129–30
"Good Schadenfreude," 48, 65–9

"Happy little 'oh wow, someone is
        fucked,'" 54

Inner peace, when someone else's
        soufflé deflates, 64
"It is not enough that I
        succeed...," 79–83, 85–6

Karmic retribution, for
    being excessively successful, 61,
        67–8, 102–3
    showing-off (esp. while
        dancing), 7, 62, 93, 95
    smugness, 44, 59–65

Mingled pleasure and sorrow,
        15, 126
Mishaps, of
    experts, 5, 8, 63
    husband, 59
    squirrels, 7

Mocking, taunting etc.,
        2, 132–4
    of sports players, 40–41

On seeing people surprised,
        insulted, etc., 29–31,
        132
Others laughing at *you*, 5, 27,
        88–91, 142

Politicians
    falling off bikes, 126
    inadvertently insulting voters
        (incl. hot mic gaffes),
        121–2
    sex scandals of, 5, 45
    unflattering photos, in,
        126
"Profound moral worthlessness,"
        Schadenfreude as
        symptom of, 6, 47–8

Quickly smothered grin
    Schadenfreude exposed
        by, 5

"Revenge of the Impotent," 10,
        117, 131–2
Reversed Schadenfreude (felt at
        own bad luck), 128
    as a British trait, 4

Rivalries
    felt toward
        colleagues, 5, 33, 75, 83,
            109–12
        friends, 83, 93–9
        siblings, 6, 77–9, 112
    Schadenfreude intensified by,
        41–2, 129

Satisfaction
    self-righteous, 5, 54
    waves of, 47, 54
"Sense of all being exceptionally
        well with the world,"
    following someone else's
        divorce, 79
Shame, 81
    mingled with pleasure, 6,
        13, 49
Superiority
    sudden twinge of, 25, 36–7, 65
    unearned, 101, 117, 130

Teachers
    Farting, 5–6 (see also: farts,
        relating to)
    Proved wrong, 72, 116
Twitter-fueled Schadenfreude,
        13, 53, 54, 128, 130,
        133, 135

Unconstructive Schadenfreude,
        8, 123
    contributing to wars, 124

Vindication, quiet, 76

Warm glow spreading, 1
Worries, relating to
        Schadenfreude
    am I addicted?, 51, 52
    am I a terrible person?,
        130
    will my friends all
        hate me?, 96

About the Author

Tiffany Watt Smith is a research fellow at the QMUL Centre for the History of the Emotions, and was also a 2014 BBC New Generation Thinker. Before choosing to pursue a path in academic research and writing, Dr. Watt Smith worked as a theater director for seven years, including stints as associate director at the Arcola Theatre and international associate director at the Royal Court. She is the author of *The Book of Human Emotions*. She lives in London.